Bones in the Sea

Time Apart on a Greek Island

by
Andrew Horton

For Sam

"Save your praise. You haven't seen *anything* yet!"
                                    –Aristophanes, *Acharnians*

And also for Argiris and Vasso

"We who had nothing shall teach them peace."
                                    –George Seferis, *Mythistorima*

Acknowledgements

This project owes much to the editing and pre-production help so generously given by Lisa Rose and Julia McSherry of the Loyola University New Orleans Office of Publications.

A special thanks to Lisa Rose and to Lou Efstathiou for their illustrations which capture so much of the spirit of both Kea and my writing.

And I appreciate the friendship and support of Dr. Charles Steiner who helped get this unusual manuscript into production.

Finally to Odette, my wife, partner, and fellow traveller to Kea over the years, for her belief in our island life and in this expression of that life.

PREFACE TO THE 2006 REPRINT

Dear Readers,

What follows is a reprint of the original version of *BONES IN THE SEA* with no re-editing or updating of facts in any way. Of course this original was written in 1987 with an afterward from 1996 when it was finally published with "news" till then.
So this brief note is an update on the 1996 note.

Kea is still one piece of paradise for us and the thousands who visit each year, and, yes, an average of 300 new homes are built a year, so the island isn't quite as unspoiled as it once was.
We also have a home now on Kea in the harbor, not up in Hora, the main village. We have a lovely view of the sea and harbor and try to spend as much time as possible each year on the island. Other changes in Kea? Of course there are now internet cafes a rental car agency, new tavernas For our family, my oldest son, Philip, is a successful actor in New York City happily married, and Sam is a University of Oklahoma student. Our daughter Caroline has begun high school and is quite a poet, guitar player and student.
The 2004 Olympics have come and gone and left everyone impressed, rightfully so, with how the Greeks "pulled it off" when so many critics were pessimistic about how all would turn out. I must add to this that Athens has changed too and become a much more exciting and human space than I judge it in these pages that follow.
And my professional situation changed in 1998 as I became The Jeanne H Smith Professor of Film and Video Studies at the University of Oklahoma. Feel free to stay in touch at ahorton@ou.edu and my web page is www.andyhorton.org. I continue to lead yearly study tours to Kea and beyond, so my web page will always have the latest trip announced.
Note that I have a second book that is half about our Family on Kea for four months in 1997 and half about our following Six months in New Zealand in 1998. It is called *LIFE WITHOUT A ZIP CODE* and is also available for $10 and $2.50 postage.
Do feel free to be in touch particularly if you have or Will visit Kea!

Andrew Horton
Norman, Oklahoma
October, 2006

****

For additional copies of BONES IN THE SEA or LIFE WITHOUT A ZIP CODE contact
Andrew Horton, 318 COLLEGE AVE. Norman, OK 73069 or ahorton@ou.edu *$10 each an $2.50 for postage.*

Contents

Bones in the Sea

Once on a long boat ride to a distant Greek island, we hit rough water. Everyone was sick, exhausted, sunburnt. When the winds finally began to drop, the ship's cook burst out of the kitchen door hauling a heavy plastic bag. He was unshaven, smoking and drunk. He sang as he dumped hundreds of bones left over from lunch from the bag into the sea. As he turned he suddenly noticed he was the sole attention of those of us–Greeks and tourists like me–sprawled around on deck. He laughed and gestured to the sea. In Greek he said, "You and me. Some day. That's what we'll be. Bones in the sea." He laughed again and returned into his sweltering kitchen leaving those of us who understood him stunned and smiling.

Like many moments in Greece over the years, this one shines brightly for me at unexpected moments.

Preface

Pikelea is Greek for a bit of this and a bit of that. It is used to describe the small plate of hors d'oeuvres served with ouzo or wine in cafes and tavernas. This book is written much in the spirit of pikelea. It's about a Greek island and life on that island today with echoes to Greek life in the past. And it is about "foreigners," in this case American, as a small family, taking time apart from the routine in our own country and spending it overseas away from such "necessities" of the twentieth century as cars, television, and telephones. But this pikelea also offers reflections I came to have about the six or more years I have now spent in Greece over the years since first arriving there in 1966. Finally, as I wrote, the book took its own shape and logic and rhythm, surprising me time and again and insisting on fictional elements to be woven in with and among actual happenings. Neither diary nor novel, screenplay nor sociological study nor autobiography, it is truly an offering of pikelea. And though I have consciously imitated no one I am aware of, I owe much to all who have written and sung well about travels in Greece from Homer to Mark Twain (Innocents Abroad), and from numerous foreign travellers of the past including the father of nonsense verse, Edward Lear, to modern authors such as Henry Miller, Patrick Fermer and Kevin Andrews, as well as Lawrence, but especially Gerald Durrell.

The time frame for our island stay was the summer and autumn of 1987.

Bones in the Sea was lived and almost a decade ago. Some of the changes over that period are captured in the "Postscript." But so much remains the same that most of these writings from 1987 hold true today.

New Orleans
January 1996

Arrival

"Christ, we're lucky," said Lou, puffing as always on a thin cigar, "no wind today, so we'll arrive on time for once."

The beat-up, old ferry boat was sliding easily towards an island, Kea, appearing out of an early summer haze. Only a handful of tourists scattered around the open deck in the late afternoon sun. And clumps of Greeks, many of them from Kea, returning home.

"And with any further luck, the contractor will have gotten the doors on the damned house," added Lou, pulling on his beer.

Lou is Greek-American, an artist, and has been living in Greece for seventeen years with his wife, Judy–also an artist–and their seven-year-old daughter, Eirene.

Kea began to come into sharp relief with bare, high slopes falling into the sea. Stone fences carving up the land like some ancient forgotten language. Small beaches tucked away within each cove. White-washed chapels dotting many of the hill and ridge tops. And like the other Cycladic islands, all of this blend of sea and barren landscape is appealing in its clean austerity.

It is the island for which I have been waiting a long time.

"What about plumbing?" I asked.

"I spent all last week riding their asses, but they finally got it done. I had to chase them out in the countryside at their other house outside the village. So you can take a crap but not a shower yet," came the reply.

I didn't care. What mattered was that after twenty-one years, I was back in Greece for more than a brief vacation. I was twenty-one when I first came in 1966. Back then I was fresh out of college with a degree in literature and about to try out my first teaching job. Viet Nam was turning ugly, Bob Kennedy and Martin Luther King had yet to die, and the Beatles' music had taken Greece by storm while Greeks were much more reserved about the international sub-culture of drugs, sex, rock 'n' roll under Aegean sunshine that was developing on the islands.

At forty-two I was coming home again.

Times had changed, Greece was different, and I had been through twenty-one years.

And I was not coming alone. Odette, my wife, and Sam, my two-year-old son, would share this time apart for six months on a Greek island. Though I had wound up spending five years teaching in Athens, and had avidly "collected" islands, visiting as many as possible, I still had not had the experience I had long contemplated: to spend enough time on one island to get to know the place, the people, the ways, the seasons.

Something more. I wanted a brief break from the twentieth century; not to bury my head in the sand, but a chance to turn down the volume on the discordant noise of contemporary urban life and international strife. I remember, for instance, that I began seriously considering time off on Kea a year before when one night outside my home in New Orleans two teenagers approached me with a 45 revolver, pointed it at my chest and in a shrill tone said, "Give us your money or we'll blow your fuckin' head off." I think they got all of twenty dollars for their efforts, but I lost some treasured photos and some more of my innocence.

Lou had just written about the small house next to his Kea summer home that he had bought in ruins and had spent the summer beginning to reconstruct, with the same painstaking love and attention he had given their present home some seven years earlier. After my anger at being held up by teenagers in my neighborhood subsided, a level of fear and freshly felt insight crept in. "Son of a bitch. I am still alive, but I could just as easily have been blown away like all those bastards we read about in the paper every day."

Odette and I talked things over that night. We love New Orleans and our old, mixed neighborhood and didn't feel like joining the swarm to the fence-and-guard-protected developments with French names even further out than the suburbs. But my sabbatical from my university was fast approaching, and Lou and Judy's new island home in a village some four miles up a mountain–where we would be without cars, a phone and a television–would be a chance we shouldn't let slip away, particularly because Sam would still not yet be in school, so he could take in this experience before beginning the long line of classrooms that stretch before every child.

The evening before we left New Orleans, friends dropped by carrying Dixie beer and Popeyes' fried chicken. Mid May and the humidity made us all feel sluggish. As we scraped paint and drank beer preparing for a tenant, jokes and questions flew.

"Okay. Six weeks on an island. But what the hell you gonna do for six months?"

"That's what we want to find out too!" Odette replied.

"Why Kea? Why not a civilized island like Rhodes? Why, you won't even have satellite dishes or hot tubs, will you?"

Paint chips and sweat began to run together despite the humble efforts of our 5,000 BTU air conditioner.

"No frills on Kea," I said. "Why Kea? I've been there before, and I like it. Not too big, not too small. Close to Athens–an hour and a half by bus and the same by boat. And it hasn't yet become an "in" island like Rhodes with its fancy hotels, discos and direct flights to various European cities."

"But you'll be with each other all the time! Don't you know how many marriages break up during long strikes, for instance, when families are suddenly with each other day after day!"

"A chance we want to take!" said Odette, reaching for another Dixie.

"And Sam. He won't have his playmates. He doesn't know Greek. I mean, swimming's fine, but what else will he do?"

"A problem," I admitted. "But we're hoping he will make new friends, have new adventures."

"So you know some Greek and you've lived there before. But that was Athens, man. You're being a hopeless romantic in dragging the family to some isolated island! Christ, they don't even have Mardi Gras there, I bet."

Everyone laughed. And Professor Longhair sang out loud on the stereo.

"We'll be home for Mardi Gras," Odette reassured our friend. And I added, "Romantic, maybe. But it will be nice to try and simplify, simplify, simplify. And to do so as a family."

And the night continued as old paint fell and new was splashed on.

⋐⋛⋗⋪⋫⋑

Odette, Sam and I by the railing. The boat approached the harbor and the village, lights already flickered on, dropping out of sight behind another ridge as we passed the lighthouse.

We felt good. Sam's eyes, which had turned pink in the pollution of Athens, were clearing up already.

A puff of cigar smoke. "Forget the view. Let's get down in the hold so we can be sure to grab seats on the bus. It fills up fast!" And holding Eirene's hand, Lou was gone.

The Lion of Kea Smiles

Kea has its fair share of ancient statues that have come to light over the years. Best known would be the handsome Kouros (young man) of Keos (7th century BC) housed in the National Museum of Athens.

But one statue is a mystery and joy unexpected: the Lion of Kea. No museum encases this happy beast. Located a country mile from the center of the village, the Lion of Kea reclines regally halfway up a steep slope, smiling at all who come to pay their respects. Carved into a huge six-meter-long rock, by an unknown artist from an unknown period, this powerful but friendly fellow holds his own secret.

6th century BC or 12th? A unique tribute to his species or part of some long forgotten cult? Nobody knows.

Yet there he is, smiling.

Hiking to sit at his weather-worn paws at dusk with Sam became a favorite end-of-day activity. His smile faces the village. Either in irony or in contentment, or perhaps both, his smile comforts. At age two and a half, Sam began to have fears about some animals. He no longer wanted his alligator book read to him, for instance. But the Lion of Kea is a friend.

There was surely a time when lions roamed Kea. And despite the abundance of water and sun and crops, life must have been hard most of the time. Surely after a brief period when the kouros statues also smiled (an Egyptian influence, so they say), Greek statues adopted the knowing, reflective, serious look reflected in the Charioteer or the famous statue of Poseidon hurling a trident.

But on Kea, and nowhere else, a stone lion smiles.

Hora

The bus, one of two on the island, is packed. We are ready to leave the port, Korissia, a slapdash collection of modern shops and houses thrown around the harbor, and head the four winding miles up the central mountain of Kea to the main village, Ioulis, better known simply as "Hora."

While tourists—Italian, French, German, British—were on board the Ioulis, few were headed for Hora. Those with knapsacks were bound for beaches to camp next to the NO CAMPING signs. (I've never heard of anyone being arrested or discouraged from camping by these Greek "blue laws.") Others climbed on a fancy little bus marked "Kea Beach," an Italian developed resort area some ten miles along the coast, and those "in-between" would find refuge in the few small hotels and increasingly numerous "pensions" springing up near the harbor and a mile further along the coast at Vourkari, a fishing village on a fine protected bay.

The early June sun was almost gone, but enough soft light remained to make out the rugged beauty of the hills and the mountain as we begin to climb.

"Those terraces! This could be China," Odette comments, as Sam pays curious attention to all of the villagers of all ages returning home on the bus. She is right. What looked like merely a bare rock of an island from a distance, turns out to be a terraced place of ingenious and hard-earned fertility.

Everywhere we look we see the stone wall-divided-terraces layering up slopes at various angles. But instead of rice paddies on each level, there are olive trees, grapes, almonds, oaks, sheep, goats, and sometimes cows. No space seems wasted, yet nowhere is there a sense of the landscape being crowded. And on top of ridge after ridge, whitewashed chapels.

Hora is not visible for most of the ride up, hidden behind several ridges. This suggests a strategic advantage for this village as for most of the main villages on Greek islands: so high up and so hidden from view by those approaching, they were safe havens throughout centuries of warfare and invasion. And so far from the sea, such locations point to another fact about island life. While sea trade and fishing are always important, agriculture has traditionally been equally significant for an island's survival.

Around another hairpin curve, and Hora spreads out in front of us. Whitewashed buildings with red tile roofs. Hundreds of houses, each a slightly different shape set at a different angle and, because of the terrain, at a slightly varied height.

The compact jumble of all this, as for so many Cycladic villages, adds up to an ever-inviting puzzle and pleasing curiosity for the eye. And the huddled togetherness of it all clearly announces that a village is a unity...of individual parts.

This is to be our home for six months.

How much a contrast in every way from the below sea-level flatness of New Orleans.

The bus edges into a tight, small plaza on the border of the village. Nikos, the driver, miraculously weaving and reversing into a precarious spot between taxis and a "grocery" pickup truck. "Hora" (from which we get "chorus") literally means "space," suggesting, of course, a peopled space set apart from other spaces. But one swiftly realizes that in such mountainous horas, space is limited, indeed. We almost needed a shoe horn to slip through the partially open door, past the truck, and onto the rock-slab road that leads up a steep incline into the heart of the village.

"I can't believe you brought so much junk," Lou intones in his gruff gravel voice. There is the pushing and shoving and lifting and pulling of bags and cases we have brought with us for our stay. "What the hell, is there a goddamn movie projector in this one?" asks Lou as he strains to lift the tan suitcase.

It was hard not to laugh. We thought we had packed lightly. But even our "essentials" somehow came to five bulky cases of one shape or another.

"A lot of it is for Sam," Odette ventured as if in explanation. Lou is already huffing along in front of us, however, and Judy is lugging another case without complaint as Eirene takes Sam by the hand to introduce him to Hora.

From the small plaza outside the village, there are only three possible entrances to Hora. One leads past the small post office to one half of the village called "Kastro" built on a hill independent from the rest of the village which clings to the main mountain slope. Another street climbs almost straight up one side of the village to the main village church and on to the local lyceum (high school) which is slightly off to one side of town.

And the main street leads under an archway much like the entrance to any medieval walled town.

Motor vehicles of any shade are happily excluded from Hora by the very nature of the twisting, narrow, stepped flat rock lanes, a blessing that automatically made the village a desirable spot to bring an active, wandering child.

But vehicles on official "business" can and do groan up the steep main street some two hundred yards into the platea, the central village square. Thus as we struggled along with our cases, we occasionally had to dodge a meat van or a motorcycle passing us by.

"What you really need," Judy added, "is a donkey!" Just then an attractive young girl, about seventeen, wearing a Snoopy T-shirt, rode by on a donkey laden with bags of flour for her family bakery.

No time to think when one is sweating and straining under the weight of two large suitcases, but I knew Judy was right. Donkeys are and always have been the answer to transportation in Hora. Everything from stoves to cases of Coca-Cola move up and down the village on the backs of the several hundred donkeys.

Past the platea, past Argiris' taverna, a few shops, winding ever upward. I do not wish ever to repeat such a hernia-inducing journey again. But we at last reached Lou and Judy's home, high up in the village, below a medium-sized church, St. Dimitri's.

Sam quickly disappeared into Eirene's room, enthralled with her and her toys.

Odette and I, however, collapsed. For Lou and Judy, who have over the years become part goat like everyone living here, the feeling was simply the usual one of being happy to escape the pollution and noise of Athens for a few more days.

Almost immediately Judy had found some mesathakia (hors d'oeuvres), and

Lou had poured ouzos all around. We sat in directors' chairs on their broad balcony with the whole Aegean at our feet.

"The view!" Odette said, breathing at a regular rate again. Lou had a cigar in hand and binoculars around his neck, peering at the darkening horizon. "The island of Makronisos is clear, but the island Evia is not visible tonight. Two tankers on the sea and one worthy tourist approaching the platea, Italian by the looks of her," reported Lou.

Whatever hardships we had endured leaving New Orleans, travelling by jet to Athens via Houston and Amsterdam with a hyped-up two year old, and trying to survive the madness of modern Athens...were suddenly worthwhile. The view, the village below, the island stretching out to the sea, the Aegean, the islands of Makronisos and Evia in the distance beyond that, and, on extremely clear days, the mainland faintly shimmering behind Makronisos. I've been on a number of balconies and visited my share of countries, but Lou and Judy's balcony on Kea tops them all. How many happy hours had been spent here on past visits. And how many more I looked forward to, both on this one and on that of his "new" house just above, which we had yet to see.

"Shall we look at the house?" I suggested.

"Hell no!" Lou barks back. "Let's eat at Argiris'. It's late, and you should see it tomorrow when you're fresh."

Our stomachs agreed though our hearts were eager to see "our" home-to-be.

Argiris' taverna was bustling with weekenders from Athens and tourists mixed in with a few local regulars. No matter. Always room for another table in the street outside. This arrangement was perfect for Sam, as well, since it meant he could do what he came to do frequently: take a bite and then run around the platea, playing with other kids, returning for other refueling stops before venturing out and away again.

Hole-in-the-wall kind of restaurant with splendid, fresh, cheap food, much like the best neighborhood places in New Orleans such as Eddie's and Liuzza's. We definitely felt at home.

Fresh grilled fish (gopes), a mountain of Greek salad topped with local capers, spicy meatballs (keftethakia), potatoes, and snails in a tomato and oil sauce, washed down with cold, raw bottled retsina wine. No feast ever tasted better, and when the bill for the whole table arrived–ten dollars–we knew that eating out at Argiris' would become a habit rather than a special treat.

That night we slept deep, untroubled sleep, as we would every night on Kea. Sam, who can be a difficult character to get down at night ("just one more story, one more game..."), was out almost as soon as we reached the house. And why wouldn't he be? The up and down exercise of the island together with fresh evening breezes and the almost complete absence of noise except for the clopping along of a donkey over there, a child singing nearby, an old man tapping his way home, all conspired against his noblest efforts to hold onto consciousness.

Statistics

Kea is a Cycladic island, oval shaped and twelve miles long with a width of six miles at the widest point. Some fifteen miles from Lavrion on the mainland, it is the nearest to Athens of the Cyclades. Its highest point is about 1800 feet. The population, which had been about 20,000 at the turn of the century and about 5,000 in 1960, is now about equal to the island's highest mountain–1800. Roughly seven hundred live in Ioulis, the capital of the island. Depending on how one defines "village," there are about ten other population clusters, half of which are located in the hilly but cultivated interior.

The main exports are meat–especially goat–milk, almonds, and honey.

The village of Ioulis has three priests, three butchers, three bakeries, three tavernas, three coffee shops (only one open year-round), a handful of grocery/general stores, one post office, one bank, one pharmacy, and one dwarf.

Kea is an eparchy which includes also the islands of Kithnos, Serifos, and Makronisos.

There are over a hundred faucetted springs and four hundred chapels.

Offices exist in Ioulis for the three main political parties: Socialists (PASOK), New Democrats (ND), and Communists (KKE).

The two buses make it possible for all children to attend school.

Every other house has a TV antenna.

All the children seem happy.

Perspectives

New Orleans is more than flat: it's sunken, below sea level. Thus, looking around, you can see left and right, front and back, but your perspective will always be from your ground level view, unless you climb a building or hire a helicopter.

One of the many pleasures of Hora, however, was the ever shifting perspective from which we saw the village. Every perspective was at a different angle, on a varying line. Looking at the village was like turning a prism in your hands or playing with a kaleidoscope.

Built into the slope of a mountain and also on a steep outcropping from the mountain–the sight of the ancient acropolis and medieval kastro–Hora has, of course, both up and down, as well as lateral perspectives and every imaginable sloping diagonal in between.

Lou is an artist with an almost architectural eye for line and division of space. And it is under his influence that I came to appreciate sitting on my balcony or his or stopping while walking around the village to simply take a look and consider the pleasing compact variety of any perspective of Hora.

The levels to the town are not totally distinct, especially because of the sloping streets and lanes. But my closest guess is that Ioulis (the town's official name) is about sixteen houses–or levels–high…not systematically from side to side, but from one extreme to the other. And to everything mentioned above, the actual bend of the mountain itself upon which the village is constructed, and the number of angles, lines and perspectives is multiplied again.

This visual pleasure the village offers is worth stressing again. Of course, the view of the island and the sea is spectacular too. One feels almost suspended in mid air.

But the town itself is an endlessly fascinating construction, both architecturally and as a human arena: stand still a moment and look around, and you cannot only see a man returning home carrying meat or children playing in the platea or women hanging out laundry or a donkey entering from above, laden with bricks for yet another building, but chances are you will also see someone else–somewhere on the other side of the village, perhaps, or maybe next door–whose eyes meet yours.

There are many ways in which a Greek village is a community rather than merely a collection of houses. And this visual contact and pleasure is one, and perhaps a more important one than is generally credited.

For example, in our travels through Yugoslavia, we noted how depressing life must be in the small villages of Voyvodina, the fertile flatlands of the autonomous section of Serbia that borders on Hungary and Rumania. These villages have one main street which is deep in mud most of the year, despite paved highways in the area. The houses face each other on either side of the road. Period. That's it. Suicide is a troublesome problem in this section, and though there are surely other causes, the visual boredom of such a village structure must have some bearing on how people view themselves and others.

As I write this, I look out the window and see my neighbor whitewashing her balcony while talking to the neighbor who lives next to us. So it goes.

Our Island Home

That next morning, espresso coffee in hand, I got a tour of our island home-to-be.

Lou led me through a small but cleverly laid-out two-room house that was roughly half completed. "I never promised it would be ready by June," he said, as he unlocked the downstairs door. And I knew myself how hard it is to get anything done on a schedule anywhere, but particularly in Greece–and especially in a village. Amesos is Greek for "immediately," a word with as much elasticity of meaning as "tomorrow" in our culture.

Living in Athens and trying to construct a new home on the ruins of an old one on Kea, Lou's hands were full for the past year. Building on the island has been undergoing a boom in the past few years. Villagers are constructing awful summer home/pensions down by the coast, and in the past five years, Athenians and foreigners have begun to buy up and rehabilitate old homes in Hora. Caught up in this flurry of construction, workers are busy, well-paid and definitely in demand.

In addition, the workers are not specialized builders. They are mostly village men who might better be described as farmers first and builders second. It's typical for a man in Hora to have property and cattle or sheep and goats and crops in the interior of the island away from the village. This means that he would also have a farmhouse, most likely electrified by now, in which he spends some of his time planting, harvesting and relaxing during hot summer days. Thus any work done in construction of one sort or another can be interrupted at any point because of the demands of farming. Of course, work may often be interrupted for other reasons, such as feast days, trips to Athens, or for the honest and frequently given excuse of "I didn't feel like coming."

After months of thinking about Kea and Lou's new house, I was excited to be entering the place at last.

Even before going in, judging from the results of his present Kea home next door, I could guess at the care and concern for detail he had already poured into the place.

Lou and Judy were "early homesteaders," according to the modern rediscovery of Kea. They bought one of the many ruins that punctuated the town in 1980 and slowly, on their own and with the aid of various workers on a subcontract job by job assignment, put together an island home that remains as close to what a simple island dwelling is like of any renovated structure I have seen.

Instead of simply keeping the house "rustic" on the outside and then filling the interior with every modern convenience, as many do in their renovations, Lou and Judy have emphasized functional simplicity. They have kept the open "one room" concept in the main room, for instance. You enter into a small kitchen which fans out into a small dining area and then into a main room with two single beds and a desk for combined living and sleeping space. This room opens onto their prize balcony, which is extra wide by Kea standards and roomy enough for many activities, from hanging out wash to handling cookouts and a large group gathering, should they ever have one. Since Greek life is basically outdoor life, the balcony is not an attachment to the house: it is definitely integral living space.

Island houses, like New Orleans traditional long, thin, wooden "shotgun" homes, are deceptive from the exterior. What seems a slither of dwelling on one level is actually a surprisingly roomy two-level affair. A bathroom is reached from inside down a stone stairway, a separate bedroom stretches off the far end of the large open room, and the "master" bedroom–complete with bathroom–lies beneath the balcony steps.

Lou and Judy have electricity, of course, and they now have flush plumbing. But from the rough whitewashed walls to the traditional wood beam roof, everything else has been kept peasant simple. Heating, for instance, is via a wood-burning stove rather than radiators or central heat. Many of the locals, of course, have quite fancy interiors these days, thus Lou and Judy's place is in many ways a throwback to more simple times, even on Kea–times that are still visible when strolling the back streets of the village and peering into open windows or doors of old folk, some of whom live in smallish one-room affairs filled with hand-carved island furniture and with walls covered with ikons and photos and bric-a-brac from long lives of memories and souvenirs.

"It was only last week that I could find the guy to put the damned doors on the place," Lou commented as we entered the new home from downstairs.

He had bought the place, as nothing but rubble, for a song. During the past year he had worked, sweated, journeyed frequently to Kea, stayed away from the beach all the previous summer, all to see and oversee the walls going up, a roof being put in place, and floors of concrete being laid. "No matter how many times you tell these guys what you want and hear them say `yes, yes, yes,' they always go and do it their own way unless you are here every day, every hour. Jesus, am I tired of it all," he complained.

His diligent grumbling has paid off, however.

Downstairs was a roomy bedroom with a three-foot-high cement platform area for a large king-sized mattress and room left over for books and such. Next to the downstairs door was also a small hall and the bathroom to the left, complete with a separated shower area and something his other house does not have: a hot water heater. "Use it sparingly," he warned. "Wait till you see what electrical bills look like here. Ha!" And he moved over to the staircase.

The stairs are a Kean masterpiece: ten steps built in the free-standing Kean stone style. "I watched the workers take a pile of stones and put the whole thing together in five hours. It was unbelievable," he added. Like the stone walls, like the stone houses for animals, like the village houses themselves, these schist stones, adroitly piled one on the other, were the main ingredient for our stairs leading up to our living room/kitchen area. Architects are often used in drawing up plans for houses these days, but for hundreds and even thousands of years, people have been building their own houses on Kea, skillfully placing one stone on top of another. Only the very "modern" houses on Kea are poorly built! These brick and concrete structures will not last as well or as long as the stone constructed Cycladic homes.

"You choose which is Sam's bed," Lou added, pointing to two built-up bed-ledges, one with an open space beneath for storage. Upstairs reflected the "one room" island house plan: a small kitchen area by the front door, and space for a table for food and my work, and the bed-couch ledges, the far one connected to the raised fireplace area; two windows looking out over the Aegean, and a kitchen window opening onto a small balcony facing the village; and a closet space in the far left corner at the head of the stairs.

"A family of eight lived here once," he mentioned, "and that's remembering that part of the downstairs would have been for the animals." Such an upstairs/downstairs arrangement is still practiced in the village, with the variation that while few continue to keep sheep and mules down below, many use the downstairs as a storage-barn space.

Lou's touch and influence were already visible all around: rounded edges instead of sharp points, the traditionally shaped fireplace, the built-in kitchen ledge with plenty of storage space below. The whole house was a model lesson in "compact but roomy." No architect designed the place for Lou. And no contractor oversaw the operation. The result has been not only a house for less than half the price it would cost on the market done the conventional way, but a customized and personalized home that, even in its half finished form, reflected warmth rather than contemporary sterility.

We sat on the couch ledges and finished our coffee.

"Early August?" I asked.

"I don't know what to tell you," was Lou's reply, as it had to be. Much needed done, from whitewashing to finishing touches in the bathroom. Final floors, including tiles upstairs, needed putting down. Lou was not finished yet, and we were not going to be waking up in our island home for some time.

Odette and I were disappointed, though Lou had always made it clear that his true guess was that the end of summer–September 1st–would be a fairer target date. "If the house is ready earlier, it's yours," he had written. But we all knew the variables of island workers and summer schedules.

And so it went. Though we spent some time at Lou and Judy's "old" place with them, and a few nights at a guest house in the village when they had Spanish guests, we took to other locales–ten days spent on Poros, some time in Athens, a few days on Kithnos, and a month visiting friends in Yugoslavia–until we could truly move into Hora.

On August 27th, when we spent our first night in our Kean home, we drank a fair amount of barrel retsina from Yannis, our local grocer forty steps downhill, and smiled big smiles like the Lion of Kea.

We had not only arrived, we had unpacked.

But our smiles were for another reason too: the house still wasn't finished–no bathroom door, no downstairs steps, no final concrete floor downstairs or tile floor upstairs…and so on.

Yet when we arrived at dusk that Thursday in late August, Lou's happy fish painted on planks of wood winked down at us from the whitewashed walls–five soothing, bright, post-primitive, playful fish upstairs alone. And so even incomplete, the house had already become a home. Sam smiled climbing on the admirable firm couch-bed mattress upstairs, "Sam's bed."

He had not been able to say that since we had left Independence Street in New Orleans three months earlier.

Yannis, the General Store

There are no supermarkets or shopping malls in Hora. Most of what you need can be found in the Greek version of the "general stores" that used to be so common a feature of rural American life. Here they are often called pandopoleions, which literally translates as "stores selling everything."

Our pandopoleion was Yannis' place, some forty steps downhill and to the left on Hermes Street.

Even on our first visit back to Kea in June, we found we needed Yannis. His shop has the same appealingly cluttered appearance of all the half dozen general stores in the village. The shop window displays religious calendars, baby shampoo, wedding cake decorations, olive oil, toothpaste, and cigarettes. Inside the often unlit (saving electricity?) interior lies a wealth of clutter carefully arranged to make sense to Yannis, his smiling wife, and his mentally slow son, Sotiris (25?).

I needed a few beers, some of his own stock of retsina wine, some diapers, yogurt, and a phone call to Athens.

"Who are you and where are you staying?" asked Yannis, a plump fellow in his late fifties and with thick glasses. His question was, of course, part curiosity and part good business. He was already reaching for the large plastic container of wine to pour via funnel into an empty plastic liter and a half water bottle.

After I introduced myself and explained that Odette and Sam and I would be around till December, he beamed a big smile, shook my hand, and made it clear that I was his friend and that anything I needed, he would provide gladly.

His son wandered in, a sweet fellow whose mental deficiency has, at least, not hindered him from working effectively around the shop.

"Sotiris, get our friend here two cold beers."

"What was that?"

"Two cold ones! You heard me. Now! Not tomorrow," Yannis half shouted in a tone one felt was his usual way of communicating with his son and which therefore did not carry the menace the tone implied.

His command to his son was also accompanied with half a hand gesture of a slap to get him on his way.

The scene was familial and comic, echoing for me a much similar father-children relationship loved in Greece. I am thinking of the ever popular Greek shadow puppet theater character Karagiozis, a Hellenized version of a similar Turkish tradition copied originally from the East. Karangyosis is a singularly unattractive, stubble-faced, hunchbacked, huge nosed, balding, shoeless, middle-aged ragamuffin...much like Yannis. He exists as a very poor Greek living under Turkish domination. His main obsession is with food and how to get it, and his battles with his family and the Turks are conflicts of guile rather than brawn. He has one oversized arm which he uses to slap his children around as the puppeteer thumps his slapstick to add a resounding echo throughout the theater, much to the roaring delight of kids everywhere. These beatings between father and children are seen as affectionate rather than as child abuse, and thus with Yannis' comic commands to his son...who went off mumbling to himself in search of beer.

And of course, like any good general store, Yannis never kept strict hours. Yes, he was closed Sunday evenings and Wednesday evenings too (a Greek law), but other nights he might stay open to 11:30 or, then again, only till 10:00 pm. More than a few times the door to the shop was open but he was at home across the street and had to be summoned, a task not easily done since he is hard of hearing and wears a huge hearing aid stuck in one ear.

His family took immediately to Sam, however. And so our efforts to keep down his sugar intake began to fall apart on Kea as Yannis or his pleasant wife would hand him a candy or a cookie every time he wandered into the store, which became more and more frequent as the days went by. "Let's go to Yannis" was one of Sam's most cherished requests.

Better than a 7-11 convenience store, Yannis literally did have everything. Early on we realized Sam needed a night light. At 10:00 one evening I descended the forty steps (it became an almost unconscious activity to measure distances by steps!) to Yannis'. He was out, but Sotiris was in. Upon hearing my short list, he disappeared into a dark back room. While I watched the late night disasters of the world on the huge black and white TV set up on top of the refrigerator, Sotiris rumbled around in back, mumbling to himself as usual.

He emerged several minutes later–after I had caught up with what new events surrounded a large scandal to which the President of the United States had stated "he could not remember"–to inform me they were out of lights.

At that instant Yannis entered still chewing his late night supper.

"What are you getting our friend?" demanded Yannis in his Karangyosis voice.

"He wants a night light, but we are out of them."

"What do you mean we are out; you just don't know how to look!"

And Yannis disappeared into the same dark hole. But after an equal period of time he came back, smiling, holding a very dusty ancient night light.

"My last one!" he said with pride.

Thus Sam slept well that night and all remaining nights that this small green light shone.

We could count on Yannis. Whether for an odd toe of garlic, a Band-Aid, a can of 3-in-1 oil, batteries for our cassette tape player, chewing gum for Sam, or just our usual fill up of our plastic wine container and a few calls to Athens (his phone has a meter on it), Yannis was there. And if he wasn't, Sotiris or his wife or his daughter and her baby–or even her husband, the governmental agriculture expert assigned to the island–was.

How many times I prolonged my conversations there just to look around some more!

Tools of every description hanging over the door, salted herrings from Norway in one corner, beads of various colors behind glass doors in an ancient wooden cabinet, gift-wrapped champagne bottles that surely had been there since the sixties, and boxes of sweets dating from long before that. Frozen chickens from Yugoslavia, and lots of shelf space devoted to school notebooks of different sizes, all with the required dark blue covers (how well stocked with notebooks all stores are in Greece!). Traps for rats next to the barrel retsina, and huge baskets of potatoes, and onions placed just outside the door.

Nothing is ever "out-of-date" here; it's just that some items get pushed further back on the shelf or demoted to the black hole out back, or even to the storeroom next door.

The only time Yannis ever showed displeasure was when we foolishly walked in carrying an easily identifiable shopping bag from a rival store. "Why did you do that, my friend?" he asked, with hurt in his eyes.

Other Islands

Kea is not my first nor, hopefully, my last Greek island.

Aigina, Poros, Spetsis, Hydra, Zakynthos, Corfu, Evia, Skiathos, Scopelos, Alonnysos, Kos, Nisseros, Symi, Rhodes, Crete, Santorini, Mykanos, Delos, Tinos, Naxos, Paros, Antiparos, Siphnos, Seriphos, Salamis, Lesbos, Chios, Andros, Samos, Ikaria, Fourni, Skyros, Ios, Siros, Kalymnos, Leros, Patmos, and Kythnos have been part of my travels too.

Like people, each is distinct, yet similarities do also exist.

Twenty-one years of voyaging to and from Greece's isles, yet one fact burns clearly: I never tire of climbing on board another aging ferryboat and watching the deck hands hoist the cables for an island I have never seen. The modern Greek poet C.P. Cavafy put it best in his twentieth-century version of Odysseus' journey, "Ithaca," when he says:

> Then pray that the road is long.
> That the summer mornings are many,
> that you will enter ports seen for the first time
> with such pleasure, with such joy!

I was truly happy on Fourni, but I hear Amorgos is fine. The village on Nisseros is my favorite, but some say the hospitality on Ithaka is special. Crete has more wild flowers than any other spot on Earth, and yet friends from Kefallinia speak of incomparable spring mornings. My summer spent on Spetsis was memorable, however, I am told that Iraklea has no hotels, no tourists, and more fish than the rest of Greece combined.

On Kea I think back over and look forward to other islands.

Argiris and Kyria Vasso

Argiris' was our favorite taverna on Kea. And Argiris himself, together with his wife, Kyria Vasso, were the two Keans we came to know best.

The taverna is a nondescript, wedge-shaped elongated affair, narrow at the street entrance and flaring out slightly at the back in the smallish kitchen. Inside, some ten small rough wooden tables line both sides and a small niche near the front entrance houses a charcoal grill where Argiris tends to lamb chops, beefteki (meatballs), grilled fish, and veal steaks. A TV set (thankfully silent most evenings) perches in the far-left corner, and the walls are covered with a mishmash of original art done by artists who have or do live from time to time on Kea, including a simple nude sketch by Lou. (Judy has not yet decided what to contribute.)

But, by extension, the street is also part of Argiris', and on any summer night three or four additional tables are scattered around the area in front of the taverna.

We take a seat on a week night after the tourist season has ended. Argiris, a lean man in his mid-forties with greying hair and kind eyes, greets us with a simple, "ya sou!" a catchall expression meaning everything from how are you to goodbye and good to see you again. He drops off a cold bottle of retsina for an old worker with a speech defect who is a regular customer and takes our order.

Kyria Vasso is, as usual, in the kitchen. She is as large as Argiris is thin, but she moves with the agility of a dancer preparing stews, salads, soups. "Kyria" means "Mrs."–a fact that once again suggests the degree to which traditional life in Greece is still a man's world: Argiris is known to all as Argiris, but Vasso is Mrs. Vasso, somebody's wife. But in practice they are very much a team, and a seemingly happy one at that.

On such slow evenings I chat with Argiris...about his background, his small village at the southern tip of the island, about Kea, about Eirene–his grown daughter seeking a beauty parlor job in Athens (yet another village

youth fleeing to the Big City) but working tables for her parents when on Kea-and, as always, when talking with Greeks, taking up all of the world's problems from time to time.

Because Kyria Vasso works the kitchen, my talks with her are limited to daytime exchanges when she sits out front with a cup of metrio, medium sweet Greek coffee.

Before the food, the wicker basket with paper napkins, bread and silverware. Argiris has, as always, acknowledged Sam by including his smallest fork. Then he is back with a standard meal: goat in lemon sauce, entosthia stew (entrails of lamb, including liver, intestine, stomach, and tongue in a rich dark brew), a mountain of Greek salad with their specialty–fresh capers–and emahm–a Turkish-Greek baked eggplant dish filled with garlic, tomato, onion, and seasonings…and a half bottle of retsina.

Simple fare indeed. And unpretentious. But every meal at Argiris' was for us more than a rival to the best places in Athens like Costayannis'.

"We will be closed tomorrow night," Argiris added.

"Trip to Athens?" I ask.

"No. A makarea for one hundred and fifty people. And somehow I have to find thirty-five kilos of fish by then!"

All of my years living in Athens and I had not heard of this old funeral custom. A makarea, as we found out and observed, is a feast given by the mourning family after the funeral. An old lady had died in a remote village that very day. And, by custom, the funeral was to be within twenty-four hours and was to be followed by the meal at Argiris'. So it happened. By late afternoon Argiris had lined up a double row of tables closely set with several dozen wine bottles in place. He had been up to our grocer, Yannis, that morning asking for fish. "Who died?" was Yannis's immediate question. Argiris never set foot in Yannis's unless he needed extra salted fish (fresh fish is hard to come by most of the year because there are so few fishermen remaining and because there are also so few fish left in Greece due to over harvesting in past years). By nine the taverna was full of relatives and friends fresh from the service in the main church, and long after midnight many of those invited were still singing, drinking, enjoying themselves. It wasn't a jazz funeral, New Orleans style, but damned close. All were acknowledging death, but celebrating the freeing of the spirit from the body at the same time.

And all of this was happening at Argiris'.

The kafeneon (coffee shop) is traditionally a village center in Greece, and it continues to be so on Kea, as well. I have seen, for instance, the special mixture of grain, nuts and honey passed out for the mnemosymna–the ceremony for the dead forty days after death–in the Kea kafeneon one Sunday.

But Argiris' taverna is also a center, not only for meals, but for meetings, for customs such as the makarea and weddings, and for gossiping farmers and grocers gathering in town on Sunday mornings once a week to buy and sell and see "what's new."

A Datsun pickup laden with goods for one of the nearby stores backs up the street to be as close as possible to the shop. Only this time they have backed right up to Argiris' door, almost smashing a young German couple with a sleeping baby sitting at an iron table outside.

The wrath of Achilles was nothing compared to the sudden storm of invectives Argiris let loose at his neighboring businessman. Veins popping in his neck, arms gesturing to the baby and the truck, voice agitated and animated and amplified to a bull-roar, Argiris the calm chef suddenly became Argiris the Defender of property and life and limb.

What I admired most in his explosion, however, was his poise under pressure. I would not have liked to have been on the receiving end of Argiris' tirade. But the fact is, in all of his ranting, Argiris never used one curse word. Not even the ever popular gamoto ("fuck it all," in English). All of his machine-gunning language was to the point: "I am in business too, you blockhead, so what right do you have to run over my customers, block my door and hog the whole street? What's the matter with you? Don't you know even the basics of common courtesy and good common sense business practice? I simply refuse to believe you can be such a stupid barbarian!"

Once the truck had beat a hasty retreat, his anger lasted all the way to the kitchen. But by the time Argiris emerged from Kyria Vasso's domain carrying a tray of lamb chops, he was smiling and laughing again.

Argiris' was part of the rhythm of our stay. Three and sometimes four times a week we were part of his family of customers, safe from invading trucks, and contented with Kyria Vasso's splendid offerings.

Both of them are from the smaller villages of the island. The only "new" taverna that has opened since they took over the taverna from another fellow is already up for sale. Despite the good business in the summer, taverna life is a hard one. Part of our pleasure therefore is the double-edged one that there will not always be an Argiris taverna, even on Kea.

First Encounter With Dionysios

Though I had lived in Greece for five years in the past, it wasn't until a particularly hot afternoon in August on Kea that I ran into Dionysios, the god of wine, drama, and of fertility, passion and irrational frenzies.

He was sitting on a stone wall under an olive tree about half a mile away from the Lion of Kea. A slim lad with longish blond hair, wearing faded jeans, a fresh Greek T-shirt which proclaimed NO PROBLEM! at a diagonal slant across the front, he was quite obviously wrapped up in listening to something through his Walkman headphones as his feet kept time with a fast beat.

We spoke in Greek, but I offer a rough translation.

"Hello."

"Hello," he answered with a smile.

"I...was wondering if you are..."

"Yes. I am," he said, continuing to listen to the music.

"Oh, boy! I'm...surprised.... No...more than that...I'm amazed to meet you...here...like this."

I was having trouble. He, however, was totally relaxed.

"Don't worry. People are generally surprised to run into me. I'm used to it."

"Yes, but I mean, after all of these years and after so many islands..."

"Why here, now, on Kea? Is that what you mean?" he said, patiently.

"Exactly."

He shrugged his shoulders.

"I guess you just haven't been looking for me. That's all."

"What do you mean?"

"I mean I've seen you. Many times. You just haven't bothered to see me. No. Maybe that's unfair. You haven't been ready to...run into me."

His feet were now settling into a slower beat.

"I'm afraid I still don't understand," I said.

"Simple. Remember, for instance, Thanksgiving day in 1966 when you climbed Mount Parnassos with some of your ninth grade students and teaching friends? Remember the homemade wine you drank the night before and poured in abundant quantities as an offering to me the next morning when you stood on top of the mountain looking out over Delphi, the Peloponnesus, and the Gulf of Corinth while standing on the highest peak of the mountain?"

"Jesus! You know all about that?"

"I was there."

"Listen. I know for a fact that you were not!"

Still a smile, never mean, just slightly ironic, he says, "Maybe you should listen. And are you sure you have any idea what a fact is anyway?"

"I would have seen you if you were there."

"Don't you remember how you got up the mountain?"

"We had a guide."

A big smile now. "Ah! You see!"

I was stunned.

"You mean that you…"

"Exactly, to use your quaint American expression. I was your guide up Parnassos, and I was the fisherman on Mykonos when you roasted a whole lamb on the beach with that group of twenty or so Australian migrant workers that next spring, and I was the old man in the field near Molimvos on the island of Lesbos who offered you water and cheese when you had been hiking all morning under a warm April sun, and…"

"This is unbelievable!" I stuttered.

"Only if you choose not to believe," he returned coolly.

"Then why is it only now, years later, that I'm finally meeting you?"

He shrugged his shoulders. "Don't know. Only you can answer that. Has to be you who has changed, not me."

"Ah! But that's not true. Sometimes you are a bull and sometimes a panther, and I know you can take just about any shape or form you wish."

He was laughing heartily now.

"Just like a teacher, even on vacation, to try and pin me down. I'm not one of your New Orleans students, you know. I'm a god, an immortal. Thought you knew that."

"But I have a point! You do change, all the time."

He waved a finger of warning at me.

"Words! You worry too much about them without actually looking behind them. Yes, I can take many forms. I can be a woman if I like and, in fact, have been. But that's form, not essence. I, Dionysios, am always Dionysios, no matter what form."

"But you belong to the past. Ancient Greece disappeared long ago."

He offered me a swig from a jug of wine, laughing again.

"The reports of my death have been greatly exaggerated."

"Hey! That's not your line. It happens to have been said by Mark Twain!"

"And who was Mark Twain if not another of my reincarnations?"

I took a long pull on the jug. The heat, the wine, the talk were all ganging up to confuse me. I was losing my grip.

"This is too much. Don't tell me you were Mark Twain."

"You said it, not me!" he laughed and went on. "The ancient Greeks passed away because they were people. The gods live on. Another drink?"

"Don't mind if I do. Just a small one."

He opened his Walkman and flipped the tape over.

"What are you listening to?"

"Bruce Springsteen."

"Bruce Springsteen?"

"Why not? Why should that surprise you? He's got a lot of my spirit in his music. I like that. And I haven't spent much time in America."

"But Greece…. This is your home!"

Laughter again.

"The wine must be going to your head. Don't you remember that Greece is not my home? I'm from Asia Minor–Lydia–originally. Greece has been my residence for longer than I care to think about. But it's time to move on."

"Why?"

"Why not? I'm restless. I've done what I could here. And besides, it gets harder and harder to live here each year."

"What do you mean? I came to Kea to get out of America for a spell. A simpler way of life, you know…."

"Yes. Kea is nice. That's why I've stopped over. But try Athens, or Rhodes or Hydra…crowded, polluted, noisy. Not my cup of…wine. Besides, they've all switched over to beer and imported wine in the cities. No good!"

I took one last swig.

"And you think America isn't polluted, dangerous, noisy?"

"True," he added, standing to meet a group of young maidens in cutoff shorts and sandals coming his way carrying tall sticks topped with pine cones and wrapped with ivy.

"But I sense the energy, the raw spirit, even the voodoo in America, and I think they may need me."

I went to hand him the jug, but he shook his head. The lead maiden, a young woman I had seen around the village previously, took him by the hand, and playfully, sportingly, began to pull him towards her spirited group.

"Enjoy the wine," he said, "and keep the deposit money on the bottle!"

"See you around!" I managed, blinded by the bright Kean sun.

"No doubt," he shouted from a distance. "No doubt."

Poppy, Penny and Poros

Because our Kea home was not destined for completion for two months, we were faced with how to spend a large part of the summer. July took care of itself, for we had already decided to visit friends in Yugoslavia.

And June swiftly took shape as almost two weeks were spent pleasantly on the island of Poros. Actually, to be precise, we stayed across the narrow bay from Poros on the mainland at Galatas.

Our Poros visit was possible thanks to the generosity of Penny, a friend who offered us the use of her parents' summer home in Galatas. While she and her husband, Costas, and their lovely daughter, Kallissa, came for a weekend while we were there, the rest of the time we were with Penny's lively and charming mother, Poppy, and Kallissa, who was staying with "Grandma" for the summer, thus escaping the heat and pollution of Athens.

If we couldn't be on Kea, Poros/Galatas was a worthy substitute...and a memorable one. It was on the long sandy beach at Galatas that Sam first swam in the sea. The nut brown boy of Kea was at that time a snow-white fellow who at first cautiously tested the water and then, before our first beach day was over, could not be dragged from the sea. We were pleased parents.

Poros and the mainland there are gentle places, the opposite in many ways of the rugged beauty of kea. In Galatas we enjoyed the calm sea of the protected bay and the lush green of the surrounding coastline renowned for its "lemon forest," an area filled with thousands of lemon trees which literally give off a lemon tang to the whole atmosphere. One radiant Sunday we sat at the one taverna high on a cliff within the forest with Penny and Costas and wondered if it was legal to feel so good.

But most special was getting to know Poppy, especially over morning coffee on her terrace/patio surrounded by lemon and olive trees and flowers everywhere, and in the evenings over wine, with the view of Poros and the open sea beyond always before us. Poppy is from Rhodesia and still speaks with a crisp British-influenced accent, in Greek as well as in English. A teacher for years at the British school in Athens, she has been retired since her husband's death a few years ago. But a more active person could hardly be imagined. She tends the Galatas house and her Athenian home, reads constantly, and still manages to spend the summer months and many other days throughout the year with her four-year-old granddaughter, Kallissa. We never tired of hearing about Rhodesia, the Rhodesian Greek community, and her shock and necessary readjustment upon moving to Greece as a young woman. "We had such an idealized view of what Greece must be like back in Rhodesia," she said, "and it was...well, a shock to arrive and realize what life in Athens was like. You know what I mean: all the dirty politics, the cheating, lying, and the need to have connections if you want anything done at all. It was all rather discouraging really!" But somehow, over the years, Poppy has kept her dignity without being stuffy, and, even more important, a kind of resilient sense of humor that carries her through every misfortune, large or small. Never did I see her, for instance, become troubled by Sam and Kallissa's squabbles, accidents, disasters.

And history, myth, and the present mixed as we picnicked with Poppy at Troizen. High up a mountain in a fertile ravine, we spread a blanket and a feast near the home of Theseus–who became King of Athens–and also near the spot where Hippolytos plunged to his death rather than give in to the seductive urges of his stepmother, Phaedra. "A perfect day," Poppy said cheerfully. And it was.

Greece Has No Culture

"Greece has no culture," Antonis Samarakis, a well-loved Greek writer friend said, as I had often heard him say, to Odette, myself, and his lovely wife, Eleni, a prominent Athenian lawyer.

After two years, it was good to see Antonis again. As one of Greece's most appreciated writers, he has had a long and successful career as a writer and spokesperson for "the common man." But he is not getting younger, and we worried about his health. But tonight he seemed fine.

Eleni, as usual, took offense at Antonis' remark. We were sitting on the balcony of their new apartment on the side of Mount Lykavitos in the center of Athens on one of our brief visits to the city. Before us in the dark shone the Acropolis with a brightly lighted Parthenon on top. "How can you say Greece has no culture? Just look at that," Eleni stated, pointing at one of the world's most impressive scenes.

"That, my dear Eleni, is the past," Antonis explained, as he has many times to many people in many places, as he refilled our wine glasses. "It belongs to another time and another culture. Greece which gave civilization to the rest of the Western world forgot to keep some for itself!" He toasts our return to Greece, chuckles and points to the forest of TV antennae that frame the view of the Acropolis.

Instead of culture, we have television and advertising and consumerism, he had told me years before.

Eleni continued, bravely attempting to defend the glory of Greece against Antonis' Socratic irony. Both had their points, of course. And another occurred clearly to me at that moment. There is in Greece, Athens, the city with half the country's population, and the rest of Greece. They are separate and distinct entities. Kea belongs to "the rest," and it just may have yet retained what Athens has long lost.

Beach Days

Until October, we swam every day on Kea. And even in October we managed beach time several days a week for brief dips. Swimming was part of the rhythm of being on an island, especially because it came to mean so much to Sam.

Our usual beach was Yialoskari, a hundred-yard stretch of sand rimmed by the coastal road between the port and the small fishing and yacht center, Vourkari, a half mile further on. Other beaches were longer, sandier, more spectacular, but Yialoskari kept a hold on us–partially because it was convenient (not counting the tar-infested beach at the port, it is the closest beach to Hora, some five miles away), but also because it was cozy. Yialoskari managed a pleasing balance between families and singles, the ancient and the handsomely young.

Many Greek beaches have become quite fancy. To be on the beach on Rhodes is not much different from the Riviera, and to try swimming on Hydra is to make sure you have a designer bathing suit and the proper sunglasses. Umbrellas, windsurfers, water scooters–you name it–have all made their way to Greek coastlines.

But Yialoskari was downright plain–a beach, a cafe/bar at one end, and trees just off the beach where scores of backpackers over the summer camped ignoring, as do the Kean authorities, the "no camping" signs.

Sam never tired of it. And so the daily trip down to the beach and back up to Hora was truly part of the rhythm of the day rather than simply a routine. On Yialoskari Beach Sam learned to "swim" with the aid of water wings, and on this beach Sam met many summer friends from various countries. He also learned the pleasures of building and destroying sand castles, of being buried in sand, and hunting for shells. And some days, there were the harmless white-clear jellyfish he enjoyed removing from the beach with a mixture of pride and disgust. Finally, on either end of the beach were the rocks–great places to go exploring for crabs and small fishes and unusual rocks and pebbles.

Sam turned golden brown–as brown as the peanut butter he devoured each day on the beach–at Yialoskari and remained so till we left. He had an even all-over tan, for he ran naked, as do most Greek children his age.

For Odette and me, the beach was a change of pace from "mountain life" in the village. It was also where we spent enjoyable hours swimming and relaxing and talking to new friends, such as the Two Sisters, and tourists from many lands.

And we got to know the beach in its many moods. There were the bone bleaching hot days when the sand was crowded with tanned Greeks and pink tourists, and golden bare-breasted women of all ages. Then there were the chilly days of October when we were the only souls about, and the water beat against the shore whipped up by strong winds.

A beach should be such a happy, simple, democratic place, and Yialoskari is. But, of course, it often set us to thinking how difficult it is to find such a beach in our own country. I am speaking again of the simplicity of the place uncluttered with the fancy trimmings that have cropped up around the world now. More important is the acceptance on Greek beaches of nude children and topless women (on more isolated beaches or even around the corner on the rocks, nude adult bathing is common). I would hate to think what would happen if the half dozen topless French teenagers we saw one day with a touring youth group happened to land on the Mississippi Gulf Coast beaches. But we have also had first-hand experience with a brand of frightening intolerance regarding toddler nudity. When we tried to climb into a university pool in New Orleans last year with an unsuited Sam, the woman guard rushed over. She was angry. "Please put a suit on that child or he cannot be permitted in the pool."

I asked her why. Of course her answer was the bureaucratic safe one. "Pool rules." There was no room for bargaining, no use in arguing.

Yialoskari was another piece of freedom for us, therefore, and for Sam. And we are all the better for it.

WKEA

Late at night the whole world comes to Kea through the radio.

Tonight I turned on my pocket-sized radio and heard Bill Haley and the Comets singing "When the Saints Go Marchin' In." It was a Bulgarian station doing a special on early rock-'n'-roll from the 1950s.

A scan of the dial suggests about seventy or more programs, most of them blurred, faded, indistinct, but there. Very few are Greek. Some are, of course,

Turkish, others from Middle Eastern countries. Voice of America sometimes comes through in strong stilted English, as does Radio Moscow and, at times, from Albania, Radio Tiranna.

A surprising majority of the stations, however, are Slavic–Yugoslav, Bulgarian, Roumanian. But then this should be no surprise: even judged by population, they are the major presence in the extended area of the balkans. And listening to these broadcasts, late at night, that's what becomes abundantly clear. Kea is not just part of Greece; it is in the Mediterranean, but even more important, the Balkans.

This fact escapes most Greeks, either because they ignore it (the older folk who have lived through two world wars, civil war and other disasters), or have not been made aware of this reality (the younger folk who are fed a steady diet of Greek culture and carefully censored history). Thus many Greek friends find it amusing but puzzling why the popular singer/poet Dionysios Savapoulos stops in the middle of one of his satirical songs to say, "I'm serious, folks. These are the Balkans!"

Kea by day appears 100% Greek. By night, radio WKEA reminds us it is Balkan and as such a fragile plaything in an ever turbulent sea of conflict.

Phil and Windmills

My twelve-year-old son, Phi,l came to Kea for a weekend in early July. In fact, I met him at the Athens Airport, and we hopped on the bus for Lavrion immediately. By sunset we were on Lou and Judy's balcony hearing about how the last weeks of six grade had gone at Phil's school near his home on Long Island.

The reunion of Sam and Phil on Kea was touching. Sam ran and jumped into Phil's arms and gave him a hug, happy to see his Big Brother who is some ten years his senior. For the five weeks Phil was with us, Sam, of course, became Phil's shadow.

I was happy that Phil could see Kea again. He had been even younger than Sam when we had come to Kea that first time during a windy, rainy March. Naturally he had no memory of the place, except via the home movie he has seen a number of times. But at nearly thirteen, Phil is now in a position to appreciate Greece, the country in which he was born back in 1974. Though he is an American, he nevertheless has the choice by Greek law to also consider Greek citizenship before he turns eighteen. This is more than an exercise in dual citizenship, for it means he will be liable for service in the Greek army should he also declare himself a Greek.

On Kea, however, such decisions were light years away.

We swam and explored and jogged and even put on our own crazy vaudeville show to celebrate the 4th of July on Lou and Judy's balcony.

But what I remember best was hiking with him late one afternoon out past the top of the town where crumbling windmills stand silent guard over Hora. "I like this place," he said simply. "We should come up here more often."

And I hope we will.

The Feast of the Panayea

August 15th is the Feast Day of the Panayea, the Virgin Mary. It is one of the biggest celebrations throughout Greece, and on the islands and in villages, it is the most important. Part of the Orthodox church calendar of feast days, this celebration—or paneyeri—is, of course, simply Christianity's absorption of a much more ancient summer harvest festival that dates back to prehistory and the worship of Mother Earth, the provider of food.

Kea was no exception.

This year the date fell on a Saturday, a happy and convenient occurrence. The island was packed. Keans living in Athens had returned, as usual, along with many distant relatives. (Hearing "Keans" discuss how Kean they are—one-fourth, one-eighth, one-sixteenth—reminds me of the on-going American situation as those claiming American Indian backgrounds struggle to prove they are at least one-sixteenth Indian!)

All day long there was the sense of "something special" in the air. People strolled around in their Sunday best. The shops, especially the butchers, were working overtime. Pickup trucks bringing vegetables and other goods were coming and going to the platea constantly. Bells rang out from chapels throughout the village. Argiris and Vasso ran to and fro, as did the folk running the taverna next to theirs on the platea.

By early evening tables and chairs filled every square foot of the platea, and the unamplified sounds of the musicians hired for the feast—two fellows from the island of Amorgos—pleasantly carried throughout the village as they practiced in the office of the Civilizing Club of Kea.

"Shall we join the feast?" I had asked Lou earlier in the day.

"Hell, no!" was his gravelly response. "I never go down. Too crowded, too noisy. I prefer the Feast of the Holy Trinity in June. There's more dancing then, fewer folk from Athens. It's a pure island celebration! More kefi."

Kefi has no direct equivalent in English. In concept, it means something like "feeling very good in a group situation" or a kind of spontaneous joy reached with good friends involved in the same activity. That is an important word, and that we don't appear to have a need to express such an experience in English does, of course, speak eloquently to yet another difference between our two cultures.

Judy agreed with Lou in principle, but suggested we go down later to hear the music, see the dancing.

Lou said, "You go. I'll watch from the balcony. Meanwhile, what do you say we charcoal grill some lamb ourselves?"

That was the plan we followed.

But while Lou was preparing the lamb, the fire, and then the lamb on the fire, I took Sam and Eirene on a stroll through some of the back lanes I had not yet explored.

There we found individualized celebrations in progress. In one small patio a table had been set up and a group of family and friends were sipping ouzo and eating mezadakia–hors d'oeuvres. Later they would join everyone else in the platea, but they were beginning the feast at home. Further along, another family was spread out over several steps of the street in front of their house, and yet another family had, since the sun had ceased to be a threat, taken up their gathering on their flat rooftop with a view of village and sea.

Teenagers had gathered on a nearby balcony, wearing the latest fashions from Athens and the movies, which means they looked almost exactly like teenagers in New Orleans or New York or London. And on the stereo a mixture of the latest Greek and international pop music.

Lou's lamb was superb. Grilled with his own mystery blend of herbs, lemon juice and whatnot, this Kean-raised meat was gone before the musicians had warmed up below in the Platea.

"They don't really get going till everyone has eaten," Judy noted. "And with such a herd, that can take hours." Indeed, from the balcony we could see the platea as I had never seen it before: packed elbow to elbow with seated, feasting islanders, with a hum of animated conversation rising to us.

As we drank our retsina, we thought of past paneyeris we had particularly enjoyed. My memories took me back to two other islands: Nisseros, a stone's throw off the Turkish coast, and Ikaria, the legendary spot where Ikarus was supposed to have fallen into the sea after flying too close to the sun with his man-made wings.

I was on Nisseros in the late 1970s staying in a friend's old family home. The Hora there is by the sea rather than up a mountain, I suspect, because Nisseros is the only remaining volcanic island in the Mediterranean that is still active. Be that as it may, the main village was still at that time totally off the tourist route, to the degree that not a single hotel existed in the town. Their paneyeri, therefore, was completely an island affair, and, even more so than Kea, a time for islanders to return not just from Athens, but from America, England, Australia –the three main homes of emigrants.

Other islands I had been on at the time of the paneyeri for the virgin, such as Spetsis, had been so acclimatized to the rhythms and needs of tourists that the feast day came and passed relatively unnoticed. But on Nisseros, however, the whole town showed up in the platea, with its ancient trees offering shade to feast, dancing, singing. The musicians that night were several old men as old as the trees they played under, dressed in traditional island costumes. One played a crude bagpipe. Everyone danced. And it seemed all the women wore red dresses, not just for the effect of a bright color, but as a token of the island's strong leanings to the Left, another island tradition on Nisseros.

How to feed so many? Simple. One price for all (of course with half price for kids). For what was about five dollars at the time (let's double that for today's equivalent), you got slabs of roast lamb–that were literally dropped on paper tablecloths in front of you without a plate–salad, bread, cheese, fruit, and wine, wine, wine.

Dawn was not far off when I found my friend's home again.

On Ikaria a few years later I had much the same experience but on a smaller scale in an extremely small village on the opposite side of the island from the main port–again, the common table, the tasty chunks of roast lamb, the set price, the local musicians playing traditional island music, and the dancing that went on throughout the night under a warm August harvest moon. I remember how pleasant it was to walk some six miles back to the seaside village I was staying in with a Swiss friend, Anna. The spirit of festivity continued as we sang our way home along that country mountainous road.

"It's a bad sign," Judy said, as we walked down to the Kea platea, "that they had to bring in musicians from another island."

"I'd think they would see them as star attractions," Odette said.

"Not really. The musicians from Kea are very good but they were paid more money to play down at the disco near Vourkari tonight, so they will be there!"

We could hear the high-pitched, plaintive whine of the violin, a characteristic of island music, as we approached.

I was, however, still thinking back to Ikaria and the genuineness of the crossroad village feast. The place was so small that there was no platea—just tables set out in the street. And I felt then how closely the great comic poet Aristophanes was to the pulse beat of such simple, country celebrations in his plays. There more clearly than anywhere else we find paneyeris joyfully carried out. In his earliest comedy that has survived, The Acharnians, Dikaiopolis, a small farmer/charcoal seller from near Athens, leads a one-man crusade for peace while Athens and its diplomats and politicians are busy fighting Sparta in the disastrous Peloponnesian War. Aristophanes' vision of what peace is like sounds just like any countryside paneyeri:

> O Phales, enter in to us,
> and join us in our songs!
> Come share our drink, and spread our joy!
> Stay up to hail the dawn.

It may seem a far distance from Aristophanes' phallic festivities in honor of Dionysios—god of grape and drama—to the Orthodox Feast of the Virgin Mary. But the connection is a strong and clear one. Simply told, the Virgin is just the latest in a long line of Vegetation Goddesses.

Whether for Dionysios or the Virgin, these feasts concern fertility, harvest, regeneration, and thus continuation. As Jane Harrison so convincingly points out in her study of Greek religion and customs, Themis, religions focus on primary needs, and one of the most basic is food. Thus it is no wonder that the earliest cultures in Greece, most especially in Crete, were worshippers of Earth Mothers in various forms, for it is the earth that feeds us.

This agricultural basis of religious custom is also clear in the ancient organization of the "year." We divide up our years according to the sun: thus four seasons and a new year in winter. But the ancients were originally followers of an earth orientation, and so had two seasons, summer and winter, divided according to the planting and harvesting of crops and tending of animals. Summer began in March, a fact reflected in the Dionysian festivals in Athens at that time during which plays were performed: as god of the grape (as well as other vegetation—especially ivy—and animals), Dionysios was directly concerned with fertility and rebirth. Drama itself, therefore, began as part of the celebration of such a "new year" coming into existence. And winter began after the summer harvest, around August 15th! I had long wondered why after the 15th Greeks wished each other "kalo heimona" ("happy winter") as they headed back to Athens from vacation. This bi-seasonal calendar is the answer. Winter always has begun in August for Greeks who have seen it that way, long before they switched first to a lunar calendar with three seasons, and then to a sun-determined division of the year. By the end of August the cafe-bar at our beach was closed, and a message in Greek and English wished everyone a "happy winter" from Savas, the owner.

As it turned out, Judy was absolutely correct.

The platea was full of happy but subdued folk. The lamb meal had by and large been consumed, and some had even asked those serving as waiters for checks, since, unlike the reasonable and democratic "one price" approach I'd encountered elsewhere, here on Kea it was every man for himself in food and in wine and beer. Conversation was lively, but no one had yet felt moved to clear away a few tables and dance.

In fact, the lack of any dance space to begin with was a bad omen that dancing would not be on the agenda this year.

The musicians played well. And a local fellow sang the alternatingly plaintive and joyous island tunes which generally sound more "Eastern" (read: Turkish) and sprightly than do mainland counterparts.

But nobody, young or old, danced.

Sam and Eirene ran around as usual, and we listened from the sidelines.

But nobody danced.

By midnight it was time for us to get Sam to bed. No one was dancing. Clapping. Or shouting. Nothing.

Now some may account for this in part to the more naturally reserved Keans, a trait celebrated and noted since ancient times when even Aristophanes in one play states a character should act "not like someone from Chios but from Keos" (the ancient name for Kea). True. I had noticed this reserve, this poise, long ago.

Yet such a total absence of the dance, that one activity which expresses the cohesion of a community better than any other, was most peculiar.

It was the next morning that we learned what Judy had feared had come to pass. Villagers upset that their own musicians had "betrayed" them for money just did not have the kefi, the feeling of group spirit and joy, to celebrate.

What should have been an all-night feast of feasts became simply a dinner in the square that ended early.

"I'm disappointed," said Sam, mastering his new word of the week.

He would have to wait a month before we enjoyed a more typical, but smaller, paneyeri.

Christo, the Milk Boy

Living on Kea, one might think that the pressing problems of the world were far away. But it is not so. Having a child here means that we needed lots of milk. And the need for milk immediately brought us face to face with the ghost of Chernobyl. Greece, like every other country affected by fallout from the Soviet nuclear power plant disaster, was ill-prepared to effectively warn its citizens how to react, what to eat, what not to drink.

Of course, people were advised only to drink canned milk in the immediate aftermath of Chernobyl. But months later it was discovered that much of the long-life milk in the paper cartons was contaminated. Apparently milk that should have been dumped when hot was not. Businessmen greedy for more profits simply packaged the milk and held it back till the "danger" had passed.

In Athens fresh milk is available in many grocery stores in the familiar milk waxed cartons. But on Kea such is not the case. Once Judy gave us a phone number of someone she knew in the village, however, our problem was solved.

Every night a twelve-year-old boy named Christo shyly knocked on our door with a fresh liter of cow's milk, still warm and still smelling of the barnyard. And each night Odette brought the milk to a near boil to protect it and us and then poured it into the handy plastic water bottle to place in the fridge.

Remember Charlie Chaplin living in his shack with his *True Love in Modern Times*? He opens the front door, a cow walks by, he squeezes a glassful of milk, and the cow goes on.

Our dairy needs on Kea were met in almost as idealistic a way.

The Simonides Civilizing Club of Kea

Simonides was the ancient lyric poet born on Kea.

The Simonides Civilizing Club of Kea is an informal organization of young folk in Hora today.

For a long time I passed by their "office" on the main street leading up to the platea, thinking, I suppose, that it was some official governmental outfit or branch.

Then on the day of the Feast of the Panayea, I noticed that the hired musicians from Amorgos, another Cycladic island, were sitting inside this office during the afternoon, drinking ouzo and practicing on a large mandolin and a small violin.

Young folk were gathered around, talking, singing, laughing.

But it wasn't until a few days later when there was a hand-scrawled poster on the bulletin board outside the office advertising a day's boat excursion to the nearby island of Siphnos that I inquired about the club.

The name tells all. Neither a church group nor a political cell, the club has adopted the island's most famous ancient "civilized" person, Simonides, as its ideal patron figurehead. But instead of being simply the Simonides Club of Kea, this bunch of youth in their late teens and early twenties have been bold enough to call themselves the "civilizing club of Kea."

I admire their vision, their innocence, their gusto.

Modern Greece has been so torn by political division, the frightening Civil War of 1945-49 being the bloodiest and most tragic example, that such a club on Kea must be seen as a refreshingly clear attempt to "keep politics out of culture." But then again, such a club, organized by youth, not old retired folk, would be unusual in any country—certainly in Louisiana where Mardi Gras clubs known as krewes remain the center of community attention.

What does this noble club do?

First, they have their club office. This small room has a happy informal air about it, totally inviting and unpretentious. A peek in reveals a couch, a table, a few old chairs, books on the shelves, posters of past events. That's it. No regular hours. But often there is bubbling talk and good humor coming from the place as local youths gather to simply be together.

But they do more.

There were, throughout the summer, excursions organized: one to Tinos, an island famous for its much visited shrine to the Virgin; Siphnos, a "quaint" Cycladic island that has been in vogue with visitors for years; and Kithnos, the island nearest Kea. How are such day trips at a modest cost "civilizing"? Simply because Kea has traditionally been one of the most isolated of Cycladic islands even though it is the closest to Athens. From most other islands it is easy to move on to yet other islands. But not so on Kea. There is one boat a week to Kithnos and no return route except back to the mainland and then to Kea again. The Simonides Club, therefore, offered an easy way for many Keans to see neighboring islands they may never have been to before, a service that indeed must help those who took advantage of the trips to see and compare life lived so close and yet so far if measured by isolation.

Art exhibits, poetry readings, culturally related talks, even soccer games were all put together by these happy youth, much of the activity falling during a two-week period they labeled the annual "Simonidia Festival."

And in early September there was a trip to Athens where dancers from Kea participated in an evening of traditional music and dance at the Lykavitos Theater before an audience of several thousand.

The club has no T-shirts for sale, no rituals, no slogans, no excluded minorities.

These spirited youths did seem to me to be living examples of what "civilizing" has always meant, in the best sense, to Greece: a living exchange of ideas and shared experiences that transcend politics and the daily crush of chores and duties.

Dare I open a Simonides branch office in New Orleans? I have not yet found an answer.

Honeymoons and Deserted Beaches

Kea was a part of our honeymoon five years ago. Choosing the island for our time in Greece this year was not pure chance, therefore, or merely practical: so close to Athens and also the island home of friends. For a blazing hot week in July back then, Odette and I explored the island, enjoyed the hospitality of Lou and Judy, and thought about our life together.

It was Odette's first Greek island, and I wanted her to have the best possible experience. Naturally, as these things go, it was a disaster. Simply put, Kea was for her unexpectedly like "roughing it." Not that she had expected the bridal suite at the Hilton. But after all of the romance travel posters luring tourists to the Greek isles, she was not prepared for a village five miles from the beach, and worse yet, a toilet that not only required the hand pouring of water into it after time spent on Lou's carved wooden seat, but, given the "dicey" plumbing on the island, also demanded that used papers be deposited in a separate enclosed waste basket.

Fortunately, our newly launched marriage survived Kea. (Our present home in Hora has a toilet that flushes with impressive torrents at the press of a button, though the covered waste basket still receives our unwanted papers.)

And the one part of our stay then that was planned to be roughing it became a pleasant memory. We hiked for four hours over trails smooth and at times impossible up and down through the region known as Pera Meria to the isolated bay of Spathi and camped for the night on a wide sandy beach under a wide starry sky while a lone fisherman hovered offshore singing and preparing his nets for the night's catch.

Neither of us is an ardent hiker. But the trip by foot to Spathi was special, for it opened to us not only the fertile treasures of the island from figs to olive groves, but it also allowed us to glimpse what Kea must have been like in the good old days, say, at the turn of the century. We learned on that excursion that the island possesses an extensive network of paths, many of them carefully laid with stone slabs and often "stepped" on slopes, and that both simple and elaborate springs seem to exist everywhere. No animal or person need go far without water on Kea. And some, such as one only a mile and a half out of Hora, bear witness to a time when large herds of animals were raised: I counted fifteen individualized drinking troughs surrounding the main fountain/spring.

Our day in the sun on the Spathi beach and our evening sipping wine and feeling the evening breeze blow in as the sun paled and sank stands out in our memories. If Spathi is this good, think of the other deserted coves and bays and beaches around the island. These we have looked forward to discovering one by one with Sam. We were pleased. On our honeymoon we had found an island where we could be alone together when we chose. And so we returned.

The Court of Two Sisters

In New Orleans The Court of Two Sisters is an old restaurant in the heart of the French Quarter, once deservedly renowned, now a tourist trap. On Kea the court of two sisters reminds us of the regal companionship we enjoyed with Poppy and Amarande.

These dynamic sisters in their mid seventies belong to the "nobility" of Kea. Their grandfather almost literally owned half the island at the turn of the century and was the best loved mayor of Kea at a time when Hora housed 20,000 inhabitants. Their father was a member of the Greek parliament. Poppy is a doctor and Amarande, a lawyer. Both are retired from official duties but not from life.

We met them at the beach, or, more precisely, on the way to and from the beach, which is how we met most of the people we came in contact with on Kea. They spend every summer until the end of September on the island in their family home, the most imposing in the village. And every day they head for the beach with Dimitri in his Mercedes taxi. Soon after making their acquaintance, we too were Merceding to and from the beach and enjoying their dry wit as they teased the not-so-swift Dimitri, a greedy, scheming and dishonest fellow who deserved all the barbs they landed.

"You are ten minutes late in picking us up, Dimitri."

"Sorry, ladies. Business."

"Business or was it lunch at Vourkari Beach?"

"Business and lunch, Kyria Poppy."

"Ah! I see. And was it a good lunch, Dimitri?"

"Lamb stew, potatoes, beans, salad, fruit. All excellent, Kyria Amarande."

"Ah! Bravo, Dimitri. And did you have some beer too?"

"Just a little one, Kyria Poppy."

Kyria means "Mrs." and neither sister is married, but even so an older Greek woman automatically becomes a kyria!

"Ah! Very good, Dimitri. And where will you go after you drop us off in the village?"

"Home to eat, Kyria Amarande. Just a little, that is."

"Ah! Excellent, Dimitri. Just a little. But your wife is such a good cook. I'm sure you will enjoy it all. Isn't that so, Dimitri?"

"Most likely, Kyria Poppy, most likely."

The poor fellow was definitely uncomfortable but not quite bright enough to know how thoroughly and subtly the sisters delighted in roasting him. Their ribbing never crossed a certain invisible line, however, since, after all, without a car and with no regular bus service after the end of August, those in the village are at the mercy of the small fleet of cabs.

On the beach, in the cab and in the village, we kept up a continuous dialogue, for the most part, about Kea, its past, and their life on it while growing up before beginning education and careers in Athens. Seldom have I met two people so animated, so young in spirit despite their age. Whether speaking to Sam and helping him collect shells on the beach, or explaining their impressions of New York and Boston (where relatives live) to Odette, their eyes and smiles and intonations were those of two sisters who find delight and surprise in all that life has to offer. For them, disappointments are transformed into humor, and pleasures expressed directly. Who could ask for more?

"Do you see that fellow over there trying to impress that topless French girl?" Amarande asks me.

I do indeed. A balding lean bronzed gigolo through and through.

"We call Greeks like him kamaki. Do you know what that means?"

"No."

"Kamaki is that long pole with a fork on the end the fishermen use to catch octopus or some fish."

"Harpoon. Spear."

"Yes! These kamaki spend their time spearing tourist girls. Last week he was with a Swede. So on and so on!"

Thus another Greek lesson. And Poppy had much history to teach.

"Do you see that narrow strip of land over there opposite us? Before the Greek War of Independence began, Admiral Lambros Katsonis cleverly escaped the Turks here. They blockaded the mouth of the bay one day to keep his six ships from going out. But at night he had his men carry the ships over that strip and put them in the sea on the other side. By dawn not a ship remained!"

But they did not spend all their beach time instructing us. Each day they would swim out a good hundred yards into deep water and float and tread water for at least half an hour before returning.

We did not do any "entertaining" on Kea, feeling that the freedom from such chores, even when pleasant, was one of the benefits of life on Kea. But several weeks after being part of the court of these two sisters, we made an exception. We were happy to cook up New Orleans beans and rice for our new-found friends.

"Beans are my favorite food since I was a little girl," beamed Poppy, and she was off again with another story of a Kea that has passed.

Work and Days

Homer has always been so important to Greek culture that it is easy to overlook Hesiod, the Boeotian farmer/writer whose *Work and Days* is a splendid record of country life and meditations on customs, morals, theology.

While Homer sings of Heroes and Kings, Hesiod tells us when to plant and when to harvest. And while Homer focuses on an epic sweep of war and peace for thousands, Hesiod documents the joys of his simple back country existence, far from Athens, further from Troy.

Together they offer something like a "balance," that often sought, seldom found, mean the ancients so often championed.

But here on Kea in a simple country village, it is Hesiod I have grown to appreciate more fully during my time apart.

And I think about the modest dictum he leaves us that we should be "knowing in birds and not overstep taboos."

Athens, City of Death

A cover of one of the leading popular magazines in Greece carried a bitterly true cartoon one week while we were on Kea. It showed black clouds of pollution hanging over Athens and various corpses being rounded up in the streets. A week before, the pollution had been so bad that one newspaper carried a front page that was completely black except for the letters "S.O.S."

Day by day, year by year, it becomes more apparent. Athens is a city of death.

In modern Athens we see much of the collapse of culture and a quality of life that is, unfortunately, increasingly becoming the norm around the world. The glory of ancient Athens had much to do with its small and thus manageable size. I do not mean to oversimplify or sound reactionary. Certainly we cannot reduce our overcrowded planet to these more ideal pre-industrial, pre-capitalistic numbers. Yet in Athens, with its four-and-a-half million inhabitants–half the population of Greece–we see the sad results of growth without planning, expansion without control.

Athens today is, as seen from Lykavitos, the small mountain in the center of the city, an endless sprawl from coast to mountain range, block after block of cheaply constructed apartment houses, miles of concrete with rarely a tree in sight. The streets cannot accommodate the traffic, the air is not fit to breathe, children have very few places to play, and the noise levels are so high that while we were in Greece a full-scale campaign was begun to educate the public on noise pollution.

Add to this the daily experiences of life in Athens: the long delays in getting anywhere, the fact that almost no one smiles on the streets, that not even the sidewalks are safe for pedestrians dodging motorcycles and cars trying to park, an every-man-for-himself attitude on the part of so many employees, especially taxi drivers who will take you only if they find it convenient.

And it was our summer in Greece that roughly a thousand people died of heat in Athens, alone. Granted, many were old folk, but the point is the city was simply not ready to cope with heat in the summer or rain in the winter (the city floods constantly with each rainstorm). The summer deaths, of course, brought world attention to Athens during that grueling month. But no solutions are found or carried out effectively.

Thus Athens grows, like a cancer, and grows, and the living dead live on till they drop.

I am being strong about this on purpose, for certainly many of our friends,

Greek and American, continue to live and function in Athens, one of the most cosmopolitan cities in the world. And, yes, there is much to see of historical interest and to do for cultural diversion there: many theaters, cinemas, galleries, shops. But life on Kea drove home to us ever more sharply how lamentable cities like Athens have become. This is not the way human beings should live. Period. There must be a better way. There has to be something better. Of course Athens offers many modern advantages and diversions. But life on Kea led us to ask every time we had to come back to "town," are such advantages worth it? Weren't we seeing that the quality of life was better outside the city despite the lack of theaters, hospitals and discos?

The Athens I knew twenty years ago was a much more enjoyable place to live. Yes, it was already too large for such a small nation, and yes, all the problems that have bloomed now were there in infancy. But there was a kind of spirit then that the beginnings of new prosperity and development would mean that Athens could become something of an exciting modern city.

Twenty years later, I find that spirit has died. No one I met spoke in encouraging tones about Athens' future. And this is the saddest sign of all that the city that has given the world so much is doomed. "Why do you come to Greece when we Greeks want to go to America?" asked a taxi driver one day. "Athens is a mess!"

"I didn't come for Athens," I replied. "We're staying on Kea."

"Kea? That's better. But what can you do there?"

"Why do you want to go to America? We've got more than our share of problems too!"

"Ah, but in America I could drive a really huge taxi!"

"What about crime?"

"I'll buy me a big pistol, then I'll have my gun and my huge car, just like in the movies!"

He was laughing, but perhaps he was serious. Clearly he had had it with Athens.

Three O'clock in the Afternoon

At three o'clock in the afternoon Kea disappears.
The streets are empty.
The kafeneon cat lies lifeless on the steps.
Lizards pant.

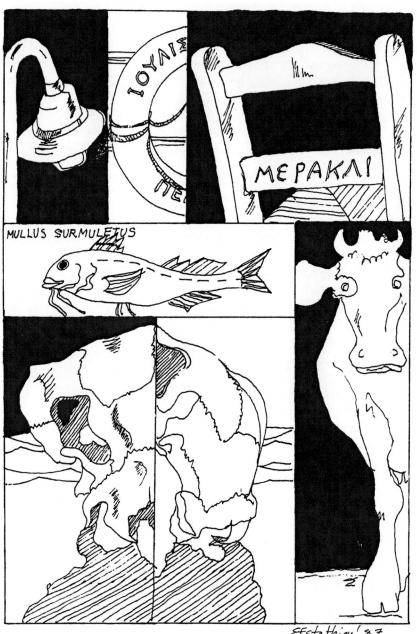

MULLUS SURMULETUS

ΜΕΡΑΚΛΙ

Efstathiou '87

The sun is molten heat.
Cicadas slow down
At three o'clock in the afternoon rocks sleep.
People are nowhere to be found.
Trees faint.
Chapels pray for relief.
Battered Toyotas pause.
Water evaporates.
At three o'clock in the afternoon
there's not a damn thing to do
but hold on
waiting
for the cool breezes of six p.m.

Voyage to Kithnos

Kithnos is next door to Kea, but it might as well be hundreds of miles away. There is no regular service between the "sister" islands even though Kithnos belongs to what was part of Kea's political domain from Roman times and is still part of Kea's religious eparchy today. I would guess that the majority of Keans have never visited the island, despite the best efforts of the Civilizing Club's excursions.

In late August we still had a few days left before we could move into our Kean home "for good." We decided on a voyage to Kithnos.

We had company.

Though as it worked out we were to go weeks without any visitors on Kea other than Lou and Judy and Eirene, that week all roads led to Kea. We had begun to become good friends with Dimitri and Katerina in Athens. He is a successful television director, and she is a talented writer and radio show host. Their good will toward us found many expressions, including the fact that they offered us their basement bedroom whenever we were in Athens. That weekend was perfect for them to come to Kea, which they had never seen, and then Kithnos.

At the same time, friends from the States arrived in Athens. Peter is Greek-American, and an old high school friend. He has become a fine playwright after having given up the teaching of prep school ancient Greek. Faye, his companion of many years, still teaches at the same prep school (math) but enjoys other pursuits as well. She had just concluded a summer dig as an amateur assigned to a Roman site south of Belgrade, Yugoslavia. They wanted to see us and Kea and Kithnos as well.

During the summer season, a boat headed to Kithnos every Sunday morning. After a pleasant evening on Kea with our friends, we boarded *The Kithnos* for Kithnos. As we pulled into the small harbor village at Kithnos–Merihas–we saw a large crowd gathered. How strange. Yes, the daily arrival of the ferry brings out the curious, but not the whole village and then some.

Once off, we learned immediately of an unfortunate accident that had occurred less than two hours before, about the time we pulled up anchor on Kea. A truck carrying bags of cement was unloading onto a small kaiki (motorized boat), had backed up too far and fallen into the harbor on top of the boat, crushing it and killing one of the two crew members. The other jumped out of the way in time. The body had already been retrieved and taken away. The crowd remained, however, stunned, saddened, confused.

We looked into the shallow water and saw the truck. It lay there on its side, ghostlike in the blue-green water.

All that day we felt the disruption this accident and this death had caused the island. It was all anyone talked about. And as is the custom, the funeral service was immediately the same evening, up in Hora–the main village, some six miles away–and the burial the next day.

Despite such an introduction, however, our three-day stay was enjoyable. Dimitri had brought his Greek assembled jeep, and so we were able to explore the island, swimming at isolated beaches, eating at other villages, following dirt roads here and there. And there was much good humor and many long discussions in our merry group of six, which swelled to larger numbers when we combined with Ariane, another friend, who happened to be on Kithnos with her friend Paul visiting an artist friend from the island. Or the group shrank as members went different ways at different times.

That first day, still under the shock of the boatman's death, we sat talking at a harbor cafe. The young owner asked where we were from, and when he heard "New Orleans," he asked if we had any cassette New Orleans music with us. As it happened, I did. I had made up my own composite tape of many of my favorite songs and musicians including Professor Longhair, James Booker, The Dirty Dozen, the Neville Brothers, and others. I lent it to him that evening, and he returned it the following morning. And that afternoon till we left we were treated to the sound of New Orleans' best music drifting out over the harbor.

It was a good feeling to be in Greece hearing James Booker in stereo on a calm August night under a full moon singing, "If I should die before I wake, I ask you, brother, to reveal my fate." Pleasing to have two worlds come together and coexist rather than clash. Fitting that Booker's words unknowingly gave expression to the Greek boatman's death. Telling too that Booker was dead, some four years before, drugs and booze, choking to death in the waiting room of Charity Hospital where he had spent so many bad nights. Yet the song remains. And Greece remains, embracing once more what is foreign, but taking it in, experiencing and learning from it too. And then finding ways to make the foreign, Greek. Thus, for instance, the blues have become not a passing musical fad in Greece, but a part of many Greek musicians' visions.

The moment we climbed aboard *The Kithnos* to leave the island several days later, a large crane was busy pulling the truck out of the water. Five minutes before the boat was ready to leave, the truck was lowered to the pavement and pushed by hand to a corner, once again surrounded by the curious. And by 4 p.m. sharp the crane was boarding the ferry to return to the mainland, its mission accomplished, while we looked on aware of having seen a circle of life and death close.

Double Jobs, Double Houses

Nobody does just one thing on Kea. Everyone seems to have several jobs. Men are farmers and construction workers. Argiris runs his taverna, his grocery shop next door, and he wanders the village selling fish. Kyria Sophia, who runs a cloth and kitchenware shop up the lane, embroiders while she waits for customers. And on and on.

The same is true of shops. Seldom are they devoted to one function or product or trade alone. The bakery sells firewood, Yannis's shop is also a telephone center, and the store next to the bus and taxi square rents videotape movies, as well as selling everything from postcards to electric stoves.

But my favorite, which doubled as the National Bank of Greece branch of Kea, was the shop next to Argiris' taverna. How pleasant that a general store was also a bank! That means you can make a deposit, cash a check and buy toilet paper and olive oil, all in one fell swoop.

How can it be counted as progress that such functions have, in our contemporary world, been separated into distinct shops and buildings? How can a dull, conservative, serious looking bank hope to compete with the inviting warmth of a shop selling cheap novels, newspapers and canned tomatoes?

On Kea, toilet paper and money exist side by side.

The Valley of Milopotamo and Philosophy

Seen from a distance, Kea is a barren, baked rock. Seen up close it is one of the most fertile places I have known. The distance between the two observations is what tends to make every Greek, past and present, a philosopher.

Just how fertile Kea could be we discovered the day we set out to pick fresh mint so that Odette could have an alternative beverage to my espresso coffee. Judy suggested we try the Valley of Milopotamo, which means the Valley of the Mills on the River.

I knew Greece turned green in winter, but I had no high hopes that in September we would have much luck finding unwithered mint. But at a bend in the road a few miles from the harbor village, we set off on foot with Sam on my shoulders. Kea is a very rocky island, but it is nourished by hundreds of springs and several streams. Thus once we rounded a bend and entered the valley by stone path, we were in another world immediately. The half a mile to the stream unexpectedly offered us blackberries, figs, quince, pears, peaches, tomatoes, cucumbers, onions and garlic, olives, pomegranates, grapes and more grapes, wheat, lettuce and cabbage, almonds and pistachio nuts, lemon trees and eggplants, potatoes and orange groves. Not to mention wild thyme, oregano, basil, bay leaves, and more. Sam's mouth was soon purple with crushed blackberries of gigantic proportion, but Odette and I were close to intoxication with the sight and smells of so much vegetation and plant life.

And once we reached the cold, clear creek, the unmistakable aroma of mint filled the air. Odette happily filled a container with leaves as Sam took off his shoes and waded in.

This area had itself been a village as recently as thirty years ago. But abandoned and ruined mills were overgrown, as were crumbling farm cottages. This hidden valley, however, gave us a clear vision of what Kea must have been like years ago. Surely this fertile land could and did support many families for centuries.

We found no more pleasant spot on the whole island.

And the knowledge of such fertility in the midst of such an apparently barren island gave pause for thought. "Things are not as they seem" is the cornerstone to all philosophy. And while Socrates and Plato especially devoted their lives to going beyond appearances in quest of the Universal Good and True, surely everyone who lives in a landscape such as Kea's learns to take life philosophically, not to accept people and things completely based on how they first seem to be.

MHN
ΠΕΤΑΤΕ
ΞΚΟΥΠΙΔΙΑ
ΣΤΙΝ
ƏΑΛΑΣΣΑ

KAHROLSUN SÖMÜRGECİ FAŞİST DİKTATÖRLÜK
YAŞAŞİN ZAZAKİSTAN BAĞİMİZLİK ve DEMOKRASİ MÜCADELEMİZ

KIZIL [R]

ANTI-TURKISH FACIST DIKTATORSHIP SLOGAN IN LAVRION
THERE IS A U.N REFUGEE CAMP IN LAVRION
WITH TURKS (COMMUNISTS) FROM FACIST TURKEY
AND BULGARIANS AND ALBANIANS FROM COMMUNIST
COUNTRIES IN THE BALCANS

Stotath— '87

Suicides and Roadside Cats

Mid September and heading back to Kea after a few days in Athens. The evening boat. This time we have the old *Ioulis*, the ferry boat on which we had first arrived on Kea, and one which looks like it may have been used in some 1930s Hollywood production in the Aegean and then sold cheap.

As we round the corner of Makronisos island, heading for the open sea to Kea, the smooth, deep, red sun is dropping almost directly behind the ancient temple of Poseidon at Sounion. Odette and I are immediately struck by the simple majesty of the moment, all the more grand because it was, like so many happenings in Greece, unexpected.

Yet in my mind, I couldn't help but see this beauty against the irony of the foreground, Makronisos. That waterless rock of a long and narrow island was for years used as one of several prison compounds for political prisoners. The bleak remains of concrete block buildings stand out against the uninhabited and uncultivated grey-brown of the island's slopes. Thousands of Greeks watched similar unblemished sunsets over Sounion while serving years for their particular beliefs about how the world might better be organized politically.

"Look at that man," Odette said, holding Sam and nodding to a shabbily clothed fellow standing by the far railing. "Do you think he's going to jump?"

"No!" I said without really thinking. People stand by railings. "What's got into Odette?" I wondered.

As it turned out, her instincts were absolutely correct. By the time the man was seated on the railing and swaying, Odette had found a crew member who came over and forcefully eased the man down from his precarious perch and then to the captain's control quarters.

As he walked into the cabin, it was clear he was a broken man. He was crying, his face melted into a desperate sob.

He was a Turk who had hit on very hard times. We never learned more. When we landed, he was still in the cabin, kept until authorities could handle him, we imagined.

But Odette was shaken. A man had almost ended his life while everyone else watched a postcard sunset over one of the most impressive of ancient temples, a temple, ironically, devoted to the prayers of mariners seeking safe passage. We could guess at the man's problems. Being a Turk in Greece is no easy road. And being a Turk in Turkey is even harder. I felt Odette's tears also came from the sharp shock of such beauty crossed with such personal pain.

Sam, quietly working on a bottle of apple juice, missed what had happened to the Turk and Odette's reaction to it. The Greeks on deck, however, most of whom were Keans returning home, took the moment immediately to heart. Both Odette and the Turk were discussed in animated terms. Yes, they worried about the Turk, but he was in the hands of the authorities. They could not speak English, but their gestures were those of "don't worry. He is alive, and if not well, at least under observation," and perhaps a bit, but only a bit of "after all, there is no reason to worry so much over someone so down and out, especially if he is a Turk."

Death, these people clearly had recognized directly and often. For them it was a case of bones that again almost joined the sea. For Odette it was more, much more. The immediacy of death and danger caught her by surprise.

It was the next day that Sam first thought about death.

Getting off the bus, we were crossing the road as usual to the beach at Yaliskari. But Sam was first to spot a dead cat beside the road. He was captivated by the sight with the clear, unsentimental absorption of a child.

The small black cat was crushed flat. Flies buzzed around, and thousands of ants trooped in and out of the eye sockets and the open mouth. Nothing could be more dead.

We tried to move onto the beach, but Sam refused. At two and a half years, he was all questions. From morning to evening he is a chorus of "whys." This time it was "Why is the cat not getting up?" "Why is he dead?" "Why are the ants there?" "Will he get up again?" "Will he be okay again?" "When will he go `meow' again?" and, several times, "Why is he dead?"

Tough questions. Odette puzzled and fumbled for answers.

Neither of us is an orthodox member of any faith, but we settled on "God will take care of him, so don't worry." That only partially worked, of course, since Sam has no clear sense of God either.

The only way we were able to get him to leave the cat and enjoy the beach and unusually calm blue sea was to tie in the cat's death with one of Sam's favorite activities on Kea, lighting candles in chapels. "We will find a chapel this evening and light a candle for the cat," Odette soothed him.

This he accepted. And we enjoyed the sun and sea and the company of the Two Sisters.

That evening as we strolled through the village and up onto the upper road taking in the sunset over the island and Aegean, we realized Sam had not mentioned the candle or the cat. If he had not brought it up, should we?

"I think so," pondered Odette. "He will be upset if he remembers later and we have not done it."

Finding a chapel was, of course, no problem. No one knows for sure, but there must be at least two hundred of them scattered around the island. A small one presented itself to us just off the main road around the bend.

One candle flickered dimly inside in the deepening dark. We went inside, and Sam carried out his familiar ritual of placing ten drachmas on the table, picking up a small brown, thin candle and lighting it from the other candle. He dedicated it to the cat, said "Amen" and we left as Sam said, "Now the cat will be okay, won't he?"

"Yes," I replied. "His spirit will be okay."

It was Sam's first brush with nonexistence, and surely not his last. But in helping him consider such a mysterious subject, we were helping ourselves as well.

Kea offered no solution but some intriguing perspectives from its past.

Simonides, the ancient lyric poet, was from Kea (Keos in those days). It was he who penned the famous epitaph for those Greeks who fell at Thermopolye fighting the Persians. Many of his best remaining works, in fact, are epitaphs. One in particular is for me memorable:

Here lies Theodoros, whose death
will please some, no doubt.
Yet the death of these will please others.
No one dodges death.

Humor, concision, clear-sightedness, and a refreshing lack of sentimentality– would that more epitaphs were as appealing.

But Kea was the sight of a disturbing ancient custom of what was apparently a voluntary (though some say legislated) form of suicide by the old. The story goes that in Roman times the population of Kea was so great–some say as many as a hundred thousand–that food shortages and famines became a serious reality. Kea was important to the Romans for its mines, and so the large population.

Suicide by hemlock (koneion) thus became a form of population control, as it was for the Eskimos even until the early twentieth century (though their old would simply go into the cold to freeze). Women as well as men would die in this self-administered way…and only on Kea, according to accounts. The whole practice is shrouded in the mist of the past, but these deaths were apparently occasions for ceremonies shared with the community, perhaps something akin to the New Orleans jazz funeral tradition.

Whatever the details, the tale remains in legend and in historical accounts that such a practice did exist on Kea.

One story has Pompey visiting the island on the way to Asia and arriving to see a festive occasion in progress. He soon learned that an old woman in her nineties was about to take hemlock. He gave an impassioned and reasoned speech about how barbaric such a custom was. Yet the woman calmly retorted, "I go from the gods of this world to those of the other." She drank her draught and peacefully asked her granddaughters to close her eyes as the poison began to reach her heart and lungs.

And another legend has it that the custom ended when a wise old man of the island–who was scheduled to die (death apparently legislated at the time)–wagered a bet with the authorities. "I believe that I can see the sun rise before anyone else." The authorities agreed that if he succeeded in doing so, he would live.

The next morning before dawn, many folk gathered on the easternmost peak of the island. The old man, however, went to the westernmost peak (together, one supposes, with some officiating authorities), and, sure enough, saw the first reflections of dawn before those in the east. Why? Because he knew that the sun's rays are projected in such a way as to pinken the West before they appear in the East.

He lived, and the logic that the old can often be as useful, if not more so, to a society prevailed. The custom was abolished.

Fact or fiction?

A living tradition, either way, on Kea.

Without Fear

The first evening with a nip of fall in it was in mid September. The next day and several weeks following that were warm again, a true Indian summer. But that particular September evening, we put on sweaters and took a walk through the upper village before going down to Argiris' for supper.

Odette bought flannel and buttons from Kyria Sophia's general store and kitchenware shop to make hand puppets for Sam. Then we stopped at a general store called Mikro Parisi–Little Paris–to buy island honey and a few other items, asking while we shopped why the place was so named. "There was a stage musical back in the 1920s written by someone from Kea, very very popular, still put on from time to time, and the title is 'The Little Paris.' That's what they called Kea in the old days!"

Around the corner we looked in at the baker in the village, one we did not frequent simply because he was out of our way, and then were invited into a woodworking shop across the street. The old mustached craftsman and his young helper were busy on some window frames, but he was happy to show Sam his impressive array of woodworking tools hanging on the wall and to give him some sample scraps of wood from the sawdust covered floor. Sam was delighted.

We wandered out of the village along the path to the Lion of Kea and climbed down to a chapel below the cemetery to go through the evening ritual of letting Sam light a candle. On the way back we had the whole village before us in the dark, made even sharper in relief by the chill in the night air. All was quiet except for a donkey braying in the distance and some radio music from a house above us.

"I feel completely without fear," Odette said as we walked along. "Do you know how good that feels?"

I did. I thought of the kids holding me up in New Orleans, of the times I've worried for Odette and the times she's told me of her fear, justly so, about going out at night, even in the car, alone or with a woman friend, and I thought about all the parental fears for Sam at home from the dangers of traffic when he plays by the house to the fears of kidnapping and worse. And those were just the personal fears; no need to start on national and international ones.

But on Kea, we were walking at night on our own as a family without fear. That doesn't seem much to ask for. But it is something hard to find in so many spots.

Yet I thought then and later that in telling others about such experiences on the island, I did not want to have them feel islands like Kea are a kind of Aegean Disney World: sterile, safe, unrealistically pure.

The recent decades have been peaceful ones, for sure. But any glance at the history of the island is a reminder that there is much blood and untold suffering tied to those who have gone before. Like the rest of Greece, Kea has been colonized, occupied, attacked, held hostage, pillaged, raped, burnt, rebuilt and sold, plagued and depopulated to be resettled once again.

Consider just one decade, 1820-1830, the time of the Greek War of Independence. In 1821, two hundred Turkish soldiers held prisoner were butchered in Hora, the spontaneous outburst of centuries of suffering under Turkish rule. In 1825, however, the Keans suffered even more under the assignment of two thousand Greek troops to the island. Rape, robbery, sacrilege were common, and one commander–Vasos Mavrovouniotis–exhibited his best manners by kidnapping an island beauty–Eleni Pangalou–and having her locked in a tower on neighboring Andros. (There is a happy ending of sorts to this particular episode: he married her and she became a heroine fighting by his side in the toughest of battles.) All of this after the plague of 1823, which killed two thousand of the seven thousand islanders at the time.

Surely fear was a daily companion for centuries on Kea as it is for us now in New Orleans and too many other places on our planet.

But, for the moment, we, like the Lion of Kea, could smile, relax and enjoy the September chill.

Lavrion

Lavrion is the coastal town from which one departs for Kea.

It is a depressing town, something like a forgotten Mexican border town or the fringes of Gary, Indiana, or both together. The old shops and houses are ready to cave in, and the new buildings are ugly beyond belief. Slag heaps from mining operations surround the town. Whores and transvestites often dot the street corners near the harbor. The graffiti is, for the most part, in Turkish, a reflection of the several hundred Turkish fishermen who have been brought in to fish since the Greeks have almost given up the profession. Half sunken tankers jut out of the sea not far from the harbor like reminders of some recent naval catastrophe. The stray dogs that lurk around look particularly skeletal.

Hard to believe that this town is the gateway to Kea. The two are a study in strong contrasts.

But in speaking of Kea, Lavrion must be mentioned since it is the starting and finishing point of all journeys to the island. This is especially true since no other passenger service reaches the island. One has to go through the Inferno of Lavrion to reach the pleasures (Paradise?!) of Kea.

Besides the ugly present, however, ancient ghosts hang over the area, for Lavrion was the center of silver mining during the height of the Classical period. In fact, without the discovery of silver at Lavrion, the miracle of the age of Pericles would never have happened. It was the financial power of this silver minted into Athenian coins that stood behind the cultural accomplishments of Athena's city. And it was the exploitation of slaves, many of whom were black (Ethiopian, for instance), that made mining possible.

Lavrion was, therefore, a hard and ugly place since its beginnings. And one senses the lack of dignity, the suffering and abuse of these countless slaves in the dismal present reality of the place. Silver is no longer mined, though archeologists have uncovered many of the shafts and foundry locations. But the presence of the Turks is a reminder of a town that has used "foreigners" to make the good life of Greeks possible. Today's Turks in Lavrion are not slaves. But they are not accepted members of the community either. At best, as one Lavrion taxi driver told me, "They are okay as long as they stick to their work and their kind."

The ancient mine shafts of Lavrion are not part of the Classical Tours that come to Greece. But the dark reality of Lavrion is also a part of the Greek experience and reality. And every journey to and from Kea brought home this point.

Stepping Stones

The workers had been saying for months that they would put in our downstairs outside steps, and on a splendid late September morning they arrived.

Eleftheri ("Freedom") is a master stone layer, and Yorgos was his assistant. As Sam and Eirene watched, silently mesmerized ("Look, Daddy, working men!"), they set about gathering stones, small and large, from around the nearby area.

No pile of stones had been delivered. This was to be a simple three-step stoop, and so materials were readily found across the street, near an unused corner between two streets, and lying next to another stone wall.

In less than an hour and a half, stones had been chosen and carefully placed and then, with a minimum of cement, wedged in tight with a seal.

This simple construction accounts for the way Keans have always lived.

At Agyia Eirene, a small dab of land jutting into the Bay of St. Nicholas, archeologists from the University of Cincinnati have excavated a Minoan trading city which flourished around 1,500 BC. The Kean museum houses some of the lovely simple pottery fragments, most of which bear the telltale "double ax" emblem which marks them as coming from Crete, the center of the rich and peaceful pre-Greek culture we have labeled "Minoan."

The excavations are open to the public, and to wander through them peering down into the stone houses and warehouses and age-old shops is to realize how little Kean architecture and building technique has changed in over three thousand years. At Agyia Eirene, the Minoan structures are built of the same Kean schist rock, piled in mortarless freestanding walls which keep the inhabitants cool in summer and warm in winter.

The purest from of this admirable architecture of the people is seen in the windowless one-story animal shelters scattered everywhere around the island. I can think of no other place I've been where animals have so many and such solid housing. It seems as if every field has a piled stone shelter, with a layer of earth on top. Most are roughly four to five feet high and thus must be entered at a stoop. With straw scattered inside, these abodes are remarkable protection from wind, storm and sun. And, of course, they suffice well for shepherds and farmers as well as occasional tourists with backpacks, too.

The stone walls of Kea, however, account for most of the piled rocks on the island. I wouldn't want to estimate how many miles of petrified fence crisscross up and down and all around the hills and valleys of this Cycladic isle–not just simple walls, many of which have no imaginable function beyond that of simply marking off individual property, but more important, the stone walls which support the many terraces built into the steep hills of Kea.

An architect friend and former student of mine in Athens, Dimitri Konstantinides, has followed in his father's, Aris Konstantinides, path in writing and lecturing on the importance of all such architecture of the simple Greek people. "Vernacular architecture," as Dimitri and his father refer to it, is another example of an ageless oral tradition handed down through the years. No plans are kept, no drawings or measurements necessary. If you need a house, you build one. If you need a wall, you raise it. It's that simple. And, judging from the Minoan houses, they last that long. Rocks of ages.

Odette on Kea

"I like the biographies of these women more than their writing," says Odette. "You really see what they had to put up with. Mary Shelley, for instance, husband dead and two children died, all by the time she was twenty-five!"

Kea was time apart for Odette too.

Reading time was part of what she enjoyed, books such as the ambitious *Norton Anthology of Women's Literature* and a pile of other books, many found in Lou and Judy's paperback collection in their home next door.

And, for both of us, time with Sam...before he started preschool when we returned. "I hate to think of him in school," she said one night late in September. "I will miss this closeness, though I know he longs to be with other kids."

In point of fact, since we had no baby-sitting possibilities on Kea, we had no choice but to be with Sam constantly. Yet instead of being a limiting chore, this necessity was a pleasure and one Odette found creative ways to enjoy (not that there weren't times we wished we didn't have to take turns in order to have quiet time: surely it would have been nice to have some time together without Sam, but in the main, all worked out surprisingly smoothly). One night she made hand puppets for Sam from cloth and buttons bought at an old lady's cloth and clothing shop up the road. And as a special treat she would throw together peanut butter (bought in Athens), honey and coconut to make Sam's favorite sweet, "peanut butter balls." Other hours were devoted to reading to/with Sam, and helping him master various games and skills. Sam's happy disposition and eager curiosity owe much to her creative and caring time spent with him, time that a working mother cannot afford.

But Kea was also time for reflection. Turning thirty on "our" island was a landmark event for her. She wants a job, and even more, a career–but what? What does someone with a general interest in the humanities and a specific degree in anthropology who happens also to be a young mother do? Many hours were given over to this question. And by her own choice, on Kea, she began to think of graduate school and teaching as the beginning of an answer.

"Svougatas are easier than they look to make," she commented one evening after cooking her first batch of a special cheese-flour-egg pancake. Odette had learned the recipe from Judy who had learned it when spending a summer years ago on Kithnos. Strange to say, though Kithnos is next door, we had never seen anyone cook them on Kea. "The secret is the cheese. It's not feta; it's ksino: not as salty, more crumbly." And Odette was proud that to buy this cheese, she had had to use some of her small Greek vocabulary to tell one of the market women on market day–Sunday–to bring a kilo of ksino the following week. "I made an appointment that I have to keep in Greek!" she beamed. "I do feel like a villager now."

Even more than I, Odette hated trips to Athens. "Why don't you go in if you have to," she said several times. "I'm perfectly content here with Sam. And, after all, he has a schedule here, and in Athens there is so little for kids to do." Our Greek friends with children have often complained about this last fact. In that sense New Orleans with its parks and French Quarter and wonderful Audubon Zoo is a kid's delight. And so, on several occasions, I did make the Athenian trip alone.

There are other memories associated with Kea. The first time I came here was a joint trip with Lou and Judy on their first trip, as well. It was 1975, a cold weekend in windy March, and my first wife, Elizabeth, a Greek, and our year-and-a-half old son, Philip, came too.

Everything should have pointed to a miserable time. We were there in the worst possible weather, almost every place was shut down for the winter, and the island was clearly not set up for casual tourists at any season.

But despite all, we had two glorious experiences. One was discovering Hora. It was a cold, rainy winter's night (March in Greece is still very much winter!), and Hora at that time was quite unspoiled and undiscovered by wealthy Athenians and offbeat foreigners. It was like walking into a Greek island village at the turn of the century.

Wandering those wet stone streets, we found only Argiris' taverna open. It was then under someone else's management (Argiris took over in 1978), but it was the same comfortable, simple, honest taverna offering shelter from the storm and splendid food. We were impressed. And while Elizabeth and I returned to the States a year later and wound up going our separate ways, Lou and Judy returned and returned and finally bought and "settled in."

The other moment remembered from that first trip to Kea is preserved on a family home movie I shot that Sunday in 8mm on Pisses (pronounced "Pieces") beach. Aimlessly driving through the island that day, we worked our way the sixteen or so kilometers down the island from Hora to Pisses, a fertile valley with a small community, the remains of one of the four ancient cities, and a fine sandy beach.

My silent jerky home movie shows a decade-younger Lou and Judy smiling while pulling their light jackets closely around themselves on the windy beach. Cut to large waves crashing against the shore. Cut to Elizabeth bundling up a red-faced Philip who begins running happily along the beach fully padded against the elements. There is also a short shot of the filmmaker, a scraggly moustache in place then and a Greek fisherman's cap keeping his long hair from blowing furiously in the wind.

What does not appear in the film is the lobster lunch we devoured at the hotel taverna, the only one on the beach. We had not expected anything to be open. But, to our surprise, not only was the owner there, by chance, for the weekend, but he happened to have on hand a few fresh lobsters a friend had caught. Sunburnt and freezing at the same time, we all greedily enjoyed a winter's feast on Kea.

That unexpected feast has helped lighten many other miserable winter stretches. "If we could find fresh lobster on a deserted beach on Kea, then..." became a happy good luck charm. And it still works.

Town Halls, Coffee Shops, and Xerox

If I had to design a town hall for a small town, anywhere, I think I might steal the plans for Hora's splendid building put up in 1900. It is located, as it should be, on the town's square, the platea. Imposing but not domineering, it is a two-storied neoclassical structure. With copies of Classical statues looking down

from the tiled roof, a grand central door and staircase leading up to the town offices and large front windows, this town hall speaks strongly and clearly of Kea at its zenith: the turn of the century.

Inside, the offices are inviting and artistically and architecturally many cuts above any town hall I've seen anywhere. There are elaborately painted ceilings in each of the four rooms (the mayor's office, the secretaries' office, a workroom containing the island's one and only Xerox machine, and a large meeting room with a magnificent oval polished wood table in the center. And every room is an art gallery for paintings, drawings and sketches by island artists and visiting artists).

But this is not all. In the meeting room is a library for the public. Books, all in Greek, range from an impressive overview of Greek culture–history and literature, right up to the present–and much of world literature in translation. Shakespeare, Balzac, Tolstoy, and Mark Twain are there, but also Harold Pinter, Proust, Samuel Beckett, and Milan Kundera. No, I never saw scores of farmers and school children in the meeting room pouring over Nikos Kazantzakis or Jean Paul Sartre, but the books do get used by those who wish to read, and even those who don't take out books must certainly feel how right it is on Kea to have a town hall that is also a library of world history and culture.

Kea's town hall offers even more.

While the front of the building announces itself as the dignified center of community government and town affairs, the rear end is the main coffee shop, kafeneon, of the town. Here in this "classical" social center the island's men gather to sip Greek coffee and ouzo and beer and talk politics and business and news, especially on Sundays–market day–the busiest day of the week. As everywhere in Greece, the kafeneon is a man's world, though two of the three employees are women, including our neighbor, Kyria Poppy.

And to find such a center within the town hall is yet another "first" for Kea!

But there is yet another entrance to the building: from the main street, on the side of the building. This small office houses the farmers' union of Kea. Here on Sunday mornings (about the only time I ever saw it open), island men came to meet and go over business regarding their farms, crops, and livestock.

Who could ask more of a town building?

No one, really, except for one more matter, which most concerned me and brought me to the offices several times a week to spend large sums of pocket money during the course of my stay.

I am speaking of the treasured Xerox machine. My writing made Xeroxing an unalterable necessity. But I was pleased that even my specific needs were met by Kea's efficient town government and its obliging young secretaries.

There was one catch, however, which made Xeroxing on Kea once again an experience different from visiting an American Xerox outlet or any photocopy office in Athens: I had to go first to the "National Bank-Grocery Store" to purchase the exact number of pages I needed and then bring them with me to the town hall.

But nevermind: a small inconvenience for the pleasure of having my papers reproduced while I browsed through the Kea public library and listened in from time to time to the mayor at work talking to happy or disgruntled villagers was no problem.

The mayor?

If the town hall of Kea serves many functions, it is only fitting that the mayor also be a man (or, perhaps someday, a woman) of several callings.

Yorghos, the mayor, is one of the four taxi drivers of Kea. What better way to stay in touch with everybody? And from all I could see, he was fulfilling his double roles with great poise and success.

A Country Panayeri

The Two Sisters tipped us off in late September that a countryside paneyeri (celebration) would take place the next day at a small hilltop chapel far down the island at Poles, the site of Karthea, one of the four ancient towns of Kea.

There was no hesitation: we had to go.

But how? Some ten miles from Hora on back-country unpaved roads and then an hour's hike down a rough path to the sea, how were we to reach this unlikely spot for a celebration and gathering?

Simple. By "school bus." And then by foot. Once the summer is over and the school year begins, the two Kean buses cease to run on any predictable schedule except on daily runs as school buses carting students from even the most remote sections of the island to Hora for school and then back home again in the afternoon. The timing, it turned out, would be perfect for our needs. Nikos would leave at 6:00 a.m. for Kato Meria, the interior village far down the island from where we would begin our hike down. And he would return at 2:30 bringing children home. We could ride back with him then.

Odette was at first skeptical. "Catch a bus before sunrise and hike for an hour downhill at dawn? And don't forget we have Sam and will have to carry him uphill on the way back!"

But once I promised to deal with Sam and explained that we were getting two trips for the price of one, she agreed, skepticism still in the corners of her eyes. "We had wanted to see the ruins of Karthea anyway. This way we get the ruins and a country celebration!"

Sam was sound asleep, a bundle of warm unconsciousness, as we walked down to the bus platea before 6:00 a.m. in the dark. The weather had begun to change, and so we wore sweaters against the early morning chill.

By the time we seated ourselves on the bus, village women, mostly middle-aged, but some younger and several in their seventies, soon appeared and climbed on board. All were headed for the paneyeri. They carried fresh cut flowers, bags of food, and containers of wine and ouzo. While we could barely open our eyes yet, let alone speak, they were laughing, bantering back and forth a mile a minute and full of kefi even before Nikos left the village.

No men? Almost. But around the corner came one of the three priests, Michaelis, a large fellow, in his black robe, stovepipe hat and carrying a briefcase, and behind him, Yorghos, his assistant and chanter, a mustached villager in his early fifties. Once the priest had regally placed himself in the front seat, the only single seat beside that of the driver on the bus, we were ready to leave.

The happy chatter and laughter of the women lasted throughout the ride and, indeed, throughout the day, both down and back up the mountain path. Of course I knew village women were of strong stock, but I did not expect them to be such indefatigable hikers and still keep their humor, their animated exchanges, their kefi going non-stop for a full day!

The interior road of the island winds through beautiful cultivated areas, rich in livestock, olive trees and especially oak trees once needed for the tanneries down on the coast, but no longer necessary. By the time we reached Kato Meria, a village made up of scattered homes, an elementary school, and a coffee shop/store, the sky had begun to turn deep orange at the horizon though the sun was not yet in sight over a calm sea.

Sam was still asleep as we set off down a mountain path towards the sea facing the island of Kythnos in the distance.

What were we headed towards? The main paneyeri had, of course, been the mid-August Feast of the Virgin, celebrated by the whole island. But there are feast days for each of the saints, and, depending on which saint a church is dedicated to, families have the chance to celebrate those days at their chapels should they choose to do so. With some 400 churches for the 1800 people of Kea, however, it is not possible to have festive gatherings at all locations.

But the family who has maintained the chapel to the Virgin at the ancient site of Karthea has, according to the Two Sisters, long sponsored their paneyeri. Sponsorship means paying for the priest and his psalter and preparing the bread and the special "food" they offer those who attend.

The dirt road quickly became an island path. And like most of the used paths of Kea, this one was constructed of stone steps, time worn, but perfectly spaced to served the needs of man and donkeys.

I consider myself in pretty good shape, but there was no way I could keep pace with the happy women who almost appeared to be jogging down mountain with packages and flowers in hand. The scenery along the way was spectacular. The sun rose as we descended. And so we were treated to ever-changing play of light and shadow across the mountains, the valleys, the sea in front of us as the light increased.

But where was the priest? A sound of hooves on stone caught my attention. And I turned to see the priest, regally seated on his donkey (provided by the family of the church), briefcase in hand, maintaining his dignity as he bounced along, the only one of our group to arrive in such luxury.

As soon as our group reached the pebble beach, the women began to climb towards the chapel on the peak of the nearest steep hill, on the site of part of ancient Karthea. We, however, held back, enjoying the view from the beach.

And then we climbed the short distance to the remains of two of the three temples erected in Classical times, one to Apollo and the other to Demeter, the goddess of the Earth and of fertility.

What to say of ancient ruins such as these? The stones themselves do not mean so much to me. But, as always in Greece, it is the combination of the location and the remains and our imagination of what it must have been like to have lived and worshiped and celebrated in the beauty of such a place over two thousand years ago that becomes a powerful feeling.

The outlines of Demeter's temple are there: modest size, simple, Classical structure, a few broken columns scattered around, flowers, weeds, and wild onions growing in and through the remains, these stones a testimony to what was but also to what passes…and is forgotten? Yes and no. Certainly the small city that was here is gone, a city that supposedly included at one time Simonides and his school for lyric poets.

But this country paneyeri is once again living testimony to some continuity, some survival of custom, ritual, belief. Instead of Demeter, it is, once again, the Virgin Mary, and, as always, it is mostly the women who carry out these celebrations. And the hopes are the same: Please, Goddess, bring us fruitful fields, healthy children, and life without war and unnecessary strife.

And something else survives here too: the beauty of the place. No factories, suburbs, apartment buildings are found here. This is the sparsely settled side of the island. In fact, if anything, Poles-Karthea is more peaceful now than then.

The group from Hora was not the only one to join the paneyeri. Local folk began to pass us on donkeys as we ascended up the steep path littered with pot shards from ancient Karthea. From the top of the hill (small mountain might be a more apt description), I could see country people arriving from several directions on donkeys, all bearing food and wine.

Inside the small whitewashed chapel, the priest and Yorghos were deep into the service. Incense filled the air, and the celebrants took turns inside the crowded church. Meanwhile, in the simple house above the chapel, the family was busy mixing the offering "food" with the help of some village women. This traditional dish can vary from occasion to occasion and from location to location and surely traces back to ancient times. But on this bright September day, it consisted of nuts, wheat berries, sugared almonds, pomegranate seeds.

Next to the chapel was a small "guest" house where chunks of fresh bread were passed out to the more than fifty people gathered. The house, a one-room structure, is there for whomever wishes to use it: two simple beds, a sink, an oil lamp, all free for travellers passing by.

Around the church outside the walled-in area were over twenty donkeys all with their brightly-colored, hand-woven saddle blankets. With the influx of local farming folk, a number of men and younger children had also arrived. And by 11:00 the service was wrapping up, and the social aspect of the occasion began.

Instead of breaking out all of the food and wine at the church as I had expected, however, most of those present ate the bread and "food" offered, and then by noon headed down to the beach. It was there in a small hall adjoining a small church by the beach that they spread out their feast and began to eat, drink, sing, and laugh.

What had been a chilly morning had become a gloriously warm noon. We took advantage of the moment to plunge into the sea as we watched ship after ship drift by between Kea and Kythnos, a main route between the islands.

When we finally got over to the hall, much wine and ouzo had been consumed, and the group had settled into some hearty renditions of favorite tunes.

Food and wine, meatballs, cheese, tomatoes, fish, bread swiftly found their way into our hands, and we were made part of the party.

With a 2:30 deadline for a return bus ride, however, what should have been a day-long feast became more like a country picnic.

But before ascending, we climbed a stone wall and looked in on the fine little ancient theater which had begun to be excavated that same summer. In the familiar semicircular stone theater, seating perhaps 200, what plays were performed? Were there travelling troupes or locals? Did Aristophanes' feisty humor set the ancient Kartheans roaring? Did Euripides' tragedies move these island folk to tears? These were not Sam's thoughts, however, but he too was impressed. Climbing down the perfectly preserved stone steps towards the orchestra he commanded, "I want my picture taken here!"

The way back was unexpectedly easy. The country folk on donkeys immediately insisted that Sam should ride with them. And so Sam was passed from donkey to donkey on the hour-long climb up, smiling all the way.

At the main road, the priest and Yorghos were already seated in the shade of a farmhouse. "What's next on our schedule, Yorghos?" asked the priest, puffing on a non-filter cigarette. "A baptism in Hora tomorrow," Yorghos responded. "Ah, at least I won't have to ride a donkey then," the priest said, clutching his briefcase as the bus emerged through a cloud of dust.

Teens of Kea

Old folk are everywhere in Hora, and every school day we could hear the cheerful shouting of elementary school kids playing in the schoolyard. But what about teenagers? What do they do on the island? What future do they have? What is life like for them?

On one return boat ride to the mainland, we met up with the mother of Prokopis, the boy Sam's age with whom Sam shared a donkey ride one day near the Lion of Kea. With her was her daughter, Evangelia, age fifteen, a dark-haired, dark-eyed, attractive young woman dressed in the style of teens everywhere: jeans, a new blouse-shirt and sweater. By appearances, Evangelia could have been a teen in Dayton, Ohio, or in Liverpool, England. On one level, teens the world over share a common culture.

But below the surface, differences emerge readily. Sitting in the chilly evening breeze, Odette and I talked with Evangelia about her life on Kea. Yes, she wanted to finish school, something that a good third of the island's children still do not do. And, no, she had no plans or even desire for the moment to leave the island. Yet she had no idea either what she would do there.

Her situation, we came to learn talking to other teens during our stay, was a typical one. The teens on Kea lack many of the outlets other teens might consider "necessities": movie theaters, cafe-clubs where they can hang out, sports events, music/pop concerts to go to. But from all we could tell, no "generation gap" was visible in an obvious way. Evangelia genuinely enjoys her life with her family, spending the winters in Hora and the summers in their country home a few miles away.

While she dresses differently than her mother would have, her life is still circumscribed by that of traditional Greek rural life: family, friends, agricultural duties, traditional gatherings, and, for entertainment, television.

Over the past forty years, Kea has lost much of its population to Athens as family after family moved into shoddy apartment buildings in the city, hoping for a better life. That trend continues, but it has definitely begun to slow down. Evangelia and others we met represent a new generation who know what a difficult nightmare Athens has become and who can appreciate what their rural environment has to offer.

But what does happen to teens today who come under so many influences their parents did not experience?

Evangelia was too young to provide any answers yet. We glimpsed some of the difficulties for those who choose to stay, however, as we got to know our baker's daughter, Margarita. A beautiful young woman of eighteen, Margarita had dropped out of school before her senior year. Extremely bright and self-taught in English to boot, she was, for "a few years," dedicated to helping out at the bakery. We often saw her, for instance, riding one of her father's donkeys bringing up sacks of flour to the shop.

Yet her desire is to be a writer.

How she will manage this on Kea is difficult to understand. She doesn't want to spend her life in the bakery. She has not finished school. "Besides being a waiter or waitress or working in a tourist shop, there are no other jobs for me," she says. Young men, on the other hand, at least can cash in on the building boom and work construction.

Margarita is, like many rural Greeks—especially women—caught in the middle.

She is as "modern" a village woman as I can imagine for village society. She plans not to work for her father, talks literature and politics with her friends, writes short stories in her spare time, and studies English too. But the traditional pressures are there: to marry, settle down, have children, and beyond all, not to live alone as a single woman.

Evangelia and Margarita are different from their parents. How far that difference will take them, and in what forms it will manifest itself, remains to be seen.

Argiris and Vasso's daughter, Eirene, also loves her island. But at age nineteen, she has moved to Athens–like so many before her, in her case–to become a hairdresser.

"But times have changed," Argiris adds. With a smile, "Who knows. People used to leave the island and never come back. Now they go and come, come and go. A few years in Athens or America or Germany, and then...back to live here again. After all, I lived in Athens eight years before settling down here once more," he adds.

Clearly such a flexible rhythm offers some hope for Kea's youth.

Cycladic Fiction

A few days after the country paneyeri at Poles, on the beach I saw some faces I recognized: two charming Greek girls (eleven and sixteen?) and their father. They were the family who own the church and sponsor this annual celebration. We had not spoken during the feast day, but we did now.

I soon learned that the father was Yannis Spandonis, a Greek journalist, editor, translator, and author. Talking about Kea and things Cycladic, he began to explain that what he enjoyed most was writing historical fiction, bringing the past to life. "In fact," he added, "I have written a Cycladic novel about Kea and many of the other islands here where European civilization began. Parts of my novel take place over 2,000 years ago."

Cycladic fiction? I was intrigued. And on my next visit to Athens, I stopped by his Halandri home where we talked further. As I left he handed me a copy of his Cycladic novel, *Kapote, Sto Aigaio* (Once, in the Aegean–1983). And I read avidly the 282 pages covering, in a kind of freewheeling narrative structure, 4,000 years and more of life on the Cycladic islands.

Yannis's basic premise shines through on each page: these islands gave to Europe a "sundrenched civilization"–all the more appropriate, as he notes, therefore, that the ancient temple at Karthea below his own church to the Virgin of Mitridiotissas was dedicated to Apollo, the god of light.

Part Kean, Yannis returns to Kea whenever possible and continues to celebrate it in prose. The past year had been a hard one for him. He had had a heart attack, bypass surgery, and had lost his wife. "I want to slow down and simplify my life. I was really doing four jobs: journalism, translating, fiction, and editing. Now I want to enjoy my life more and write more fiction. Kea helps me do this!"

I agreed.

Simonides Civilizing Club Announcement

The Simonides Civilizing Club of Kea posted the following announcement around Hora in late September:

THE CIVILIZING CLUB OFFERS ENGLISH LESSONS
BEGINNING OCTOBER 1ST AT 7-9 PM AND EVERY
THURSDAY EVENING AFTERWARDS IN THE LYCEUM
TO BE TAUGHT BY OUR NEW SCHOOL TEACHER:
KADONI NIKOLAOU

In Praise of Almonds

I grew up on black walnuts. They grew in my grandparents' yard in Virginia. During the years I lived in Greece, however, I came to switch allegiance to pistachios. Then New Orleans seduced me with peanuts, even the back-country tradition of soggy boiled peanuts. Ah, yes. And I almost forgot pecans. As a kid, I lived a few years in the pecan capitol of the world: Albany, Georgia.

But on Kea, it's almonds: almonds by the kilo, the sackful, a rooftop full, on the trees, drying in the sun, yielding up their fruit to a delicate hammer blow.

Yes, I've eaten hundreds of Hershey almond chocolate bars, and Louisiana trout almandine is splendid.

Yet Kea has given me the lusty experience of eating fresh almonds till I am full or tired of hammering or both.

And I was afraid I might have missed them altogether. Though by late September we saw Keans harvesting these aristocratic nuts and raking them out on rooftops in the sun, nobody seemed sure where we could buy them. Then on a walk from Hora to the port one day we saw a large old fellow, a Greek Falstaff of a man with a bushy moustache, shelling them in his garden. We asked, and he obliged. Two kilos, and we went through them in a few days. Thus there were other trips to visit Pericles, who laughed heartily and was pleased that we were pleased and that, as usual, Sam insisted on being the one to pay.

Can I readjust to peanuts again when we leave? Surely the memory of Kean almonds will remain every time I see the expensive price tag on shelled and slivered almonds encased in plastic in American shops.

Sam Grows

On September 30th, Sam became two-and-a-half years old. No party, but Odette and I thought about his passage from toddler to preschooler.

That Sam was not yet of school age was a major factor in our decision to spend so much time on an island. When else would we have the time? This was our chance, and our Kea stay was every bit as much his time as ours. We had worried some before coming if he would do well without his New Orleans friends, home, rhythm. But he settled into Kea almost immediately. His days till October had an unhurried order to them as he rose by about 9:00, breakfasted and headed for the beach by 10:00 or 10:30. There he explored, played, swam, often with other kids–Scottish, French, Greek, German, and American–whom he met there. At home again in the early afternoon after running errands such as stopping in the bakery to buy a kilo of bread, which he usually insisted on carrying halfway up the way home and then turned over to us, we lunched. Siesta followed, usually for two to three hours. Then it was time to play, to go for water at the spring above our home some two hundred yards, ride his red Greek tricycle around St. Dimitrios' church up the slope from us, or go for long afternoon-evening strolls through the village and along country lanes. Supper was either at home or at Argiris', and then came the leisurely preparations for bed: stories, play, a last bottle of apple juice or fresh cow's milk from Christo's cows. Bedtime was usually around 11:00 simply because dinner is later in Greece, but also because Sam, like Odette, is a born night person who doesn't want to miss a thing. He seldom went to sleep: he would just stop being awake.

Kea through his eyes?

Donkeys everywhere instead of cars. And rides on donkeys from time to time. The first time was near the Lion of Kea, and he loved it. At one point he looked up and said, "Look Mommy, donkeys go by themselves. They don't have steering wheels."

Old ladies constantly making a fuss over him. At first he hated this violation of personal space for they insisted on being right up in his face with their "Ah, what a sweet boy" cooing. So he slapped a few of them, a fact that caused us some bad will temporarily. But he learned to deal with them and even to indulge them. While they muttered on to him in Greek, he nodded in agreement and would say, "nai, nai" (yes, yes).

The glories of the beach. Which included becoming friendly with the sea, for in New Orleans, though we have a large lake on one side and the Mississippi River on another, there is no place other than pools in which to swim because of pollution. He didn't learn to swim exactly, but he had no fear of the water, and with his plastic inflated arm bands, he would have paddled off to Lavrion if we had not pulled him back time after time. Besides meeting other children and building sand castles and finding shells and swimming, the beach offered other surprises from time to time, particularly in the form of harmless jellyfish which invaded Kea a few times. He got great pleasure out of picking them up with a plastic shovel and dumping them on the other side of the beach away from bathers.

His friendship with Eirene. Though she was more than five years older, she was good about letting Sam tag along with and behind her. And whenever she would leave to return to Athens, Sam would go through his "I miss Eirene" phase.

Lighting candles in small chapels was, however, a memory he may well keep over the years. Everyday we gave him ten drachmas when he entered any one of the many chapels in Hora or in the countryside. His routine was set. He'd put the money in the candle coin box, pick up a small dark brown candle and light it either from the "eternal flame" (simple olive oil affairs in a glass) or from matches provided, place it in the candle holder, say "Amen," and announce to whom that day's candle had been dedicated. Many were for my grandmother, his great-grandmother, ninety-three at the time. Others were for other family members and friends. But it was always easy to motivate him for a walk by saying the magic phrase, "let's go light a candle."

The platea was a favorite haunt as well. There other kids gathered. There he could run and climb and hide. There he could divide his time checking on what was going on and then running back to Argiris' to eat. So many village children knew him that after awhile we did not automatically jump up to look after him every time he disappeared from sight of the taverna. Only when the foreign sound of a truck or motorcycle broke the silence of Hora did we go running after him.

But what convinced us that Sam had arrived as a preschooler was not just his leaps and bounds with picking up new words, new thought patterns, new game skills, new physical abilities, new attitudes, though these were signs too. It was his sudden determination that he wanted to go to school.

How did this come about? Because by September, Eirene left for school. "I want to go to school too," he said dozens of times a day. And we assured him that indeed when we returned to New Orleans, he too would have a lunch pail and a schoolbag and would leave home each day and return later with stories of what he had done at preschool that day. "I'm a big boy now" also became a key phrase on Kea. And it was so. On Kea Sam began to grow up.

And as Sam thought of school, he often sang "Mary Had a Little Lamb." There are, of course, many lambs on Kea, thus it made good sense that a lamb might follow him to school. "I will go to school in New Orleans," he would say, "and a lamb will follow me!" To which Odette would add, "Well, I'm not sure if that will happen, because there aren't as many lambs in New Orleans as on Kea."

"Oh," said Sam, packing a bag we called his "schoolbag."

The Bronze Age, the Sixties, the Seventies, and the Present

Living on Kea was not just the opposite of living in Athens. For me it was also coming to an awareness of Greece as I used to know it and Greece now.

I arrived in 1966, and by the time I had learned some Greek and begun to feel comfortable and to know my way around, the military dictatorship of Colonel Papadopoulos came into swift power on April 21, 1967. I lived for the next year under the Junta and saw the changes it wrought in the country and returned several summers during its seven-year rule. And in 1973, Ph.D. in hand, I returned to live in Greece, thereby experiencing the downfall of military rule and the triumphant joy of the return to freedom during the summer of 1974.

Thus on a political level, my time on Kea in the 1980s brought home to me the shape and feeling of the entire cycle of Greek political life. The Greeks are proud of pointing out that no tyranny has lasted for long in Greece, which is true. But also true are the turbulent phases of democracy that also collapse and have collapsed over the years due to factionism, greed, uncompromising ideological stances, and all of the other complicated reasons that keep people everywhere from getting along smoothly.

Yet Greece today has a democratic government no longer burdened with an imposed monarchy (it was voted out shortly after the Junta) or a dictatorship.

But what was it like to live under a Junta?

As a young American abroad, I found the Junta period to be an intense and often passionate time to live. That time was a period of political initiation for me, for up till then, politics had seemed to me something distant, boring, unrelated to my own life. In my last years of college, of course, I began to realize that being against the war in Viet Nam was involving me in very practical politics. But in 1966, protests were limited and, after all, my draft board had given me permission to teach in Greece.

Think of the shock, therefore, when the six of us college grads teaching at Athens College for a year woke up that April morning in 1967 to hear that the bloodless coup had taken place, tanks were in the street, and that anyone on the streets after sunset would be shot. Suddenly politics became part of daily life for all of us. And as Americans we were "outraged" that the Greek coup applied to us as well, we who lived under a constitution guaranteeing liberty and freedom to all. I remember long discussions into the night between the six of us and our Greek friends about everything related to the military, government rule, and change.

Greece taught us a lot quickly in those days. The day after the Coup, travel was permitted again, and our gang of six took off for Spring Break on Crete. What we found everywhere was a spirit of depression, caution, sadness. Crete is Greece magnified. It is to Greece what Texas is, at least in myth, to the United States. Everything is bigger, stronger, better, brighter, darker there. After all, Zorba the Greek and his creator, Nikos Kazantzakis, were from Crete, that largest of Greek islands, situated between Europe and the Middle East/Africa where European civilization began.

The people of Crete are freedom lovers, and they were definitely upset that the Colonels had taken over. In the worst drinking bout of my life, we shared the sadness of a group of Cretan men in a small bar in Aghios Lukas, drinking over fifteen ouzos while consuming platefuls of snails. The men had taken to the hills that day to bury their rifles so the police, who were rounding up all guns, would not find them. Many of their friends had been arrested that day as well, and no one knew what would happen. All they knew was that their fathers had fought Turks on Crete, and they had killed Germans in one of the most daring and prolonged battles of World War II (the Battle of Crete: the Germans against Cretan peasants and some soldiers and some British cost Hitler his African campaign). The result was that most of the island became socialist if not communist (Crete voted eighty-seven percent socialist in the national elections of 1985), and the Junta knew it would have to round up as many Cretan leaders as possible if it was to survive.

Thus in my mind, the bitter years of Viet Nam are mixed with the immediate reality of living under tyranny. But there was one huge difference. Viet Nam was fought over there and the Junta was visible everywhere, particularly after the leaders hired a Madison Avenue ad agency, designed a striking logo of a soldier standing in front of a flaming phoenix, and plastered Greece with the emblem, even placing it on all matchboxes.

After the nervous excitement of the initial days and weeks, however, the more important lessons I learned came from how people acted and reacted on a day-to-day basis. Again as an idealistic and naive American, I half expected a secret resistance army to be formed and to start literally battling tyranny. Resistance groups were formed around the world, and they did publicize the tortures committed by the Colonels and the ruling follies of many of their policies. But a surprising (to me) number of people simply went about their everyday life almost as if nothing had happened.

Why? Why no resistance attacks on military positions, why so few leaflets in the streets, so few efforts at organizing resistance?

Two large reasons became clear. First, I began to learn what I knew too little about: the Greek Civil War of 1945-1949. Almost a million Greeks killed each other in this cruel war that followed immediately on the tragic sufferings of World War II. For too many Greeks in 1967, these wounds and memories had not healed, and they did not want to risk another era of bloodshed. They had suffered and survived and fought or made their compromises, and they preferred, at least in the first two years, to "wait and see" what would happen.

I have many memories of long conversations and attempted conversations with Greeks about the Civil War that broke off because the memories were too strong, an event so horrible that no true history of the war yet exists, though popular books such as Nicholas Gage's *Eleni* have taken one side or the other in dealing with the micro sections of that war.

Once on a boat returning from Paros, I talked with a striking white-haired man who closely resembled Spencer Tracy. I had to ask questions to get answers because he was quiet spoken and modest. But what unfolded was a story of over twenty years spent in one prison or another, always for political reasons. He was, of course, a communist. Was he bitter that the 'other' side won and that he had lost the 'best' years of his life? He smiled.

"Why should I be bitter? I met my wife in prison. We were married in prison. Many of my best friendships were made there. I read so many books I treasure during that time. And besides, I am patient. The 'other side,' as you say, is in power now. But all things change. Heraclitus is right. All is flux. And I believe in Marx's philosophy, so I can afford to wait. Our time will come. Only the short-sighted are in a hurry!"

He smiled again and offered me a cigarette.

In the small museum in Kea there are Neolithic and Bronze Age pots and tools. They go back almost 6,000 years. The more I visited the museum, the more I bypassed the Classical period room and went straight to the second floor where the Bronze Age and Minoan period were housed. We know a lot about the

Classical Greeks. They left us and wrote us so much. But we don't know a tenth of what we would like to know about these earlier people.

Being on Kea and in Greece does force one to think about and begin to feel to what thousands of years of human history and life and politics adds up. The ex-prisoner on the boat from Paros had that kind of calm that can only come from taking such a long view. And it's a form of patience and serenity that is hard or impossible to attain in the United States. Our history is too short, and our focus is too intensely on the here and now and even, perhaps, more so on tomorrow.

Yet in 1967 and after, others were quiet because they were pleased with the Junta. That was another valuable lesson to me. Juntas don't rule by force alone. They have followers and friends. Yes, in the first few years the political prisons, including the island opposite Kea–Makronisos–were full and torture did go on, but many people were happy that "law and order" was restored. Inflation was curbed, prostitutes put out of business, roads in rural areas constructed, and isolated villages electrified for the first time. And low-interest loans were made to farmers and to families wishing to build new homes or add onto present dwellings. Suddenly there was full employment and construction everywhere. The Junta was living way beyond its means in these loans, but it helped to win support, especially in the villages, a fact that pleased Papadopoulos, a villager himself.

I lost a lot of innocence during those years. Friends I thought were friends turned out to be hypocrites or worse. Others who were quiet I learned were in the Resistance and taking chances daily. And others, I came to realize and accept, were clearly and honestly in the middle–neither with the Colonels but not able or willing to risk all that would need to be risked to fight them. Finally I realized what a strange position we as foreigners were in. Was it right to become too passionately involved in Greek politics if we were not also working for an improved America as well? I particularly became suspicious of several American colleagues who made a dramatic and visible show of their support for the Resistance while doing nothing for or against any of the many problems facing the United States at the time. The fact that they subsequently were given twenty-four hours to get out of the country by the military police once their leaflet publishing activities were known–a getaway written up in international papers–only increased my questioning of their motives. Sure, the Greek War of Independence (1821-1826) might not have been won or at least not as soon if not for the organizational and military skills and money and support of the Philhellines. But those foreigners, like the American George Jarvis and England's

Lord Byron, knew they were engaged in a life or death struggle, while my teaching colleagues who were expelled from Greece knew that the Junta was not likely to jail Americans.

The result was that while I did what I could in quietly helping the anti-Junta effort, by the spring of 1968, I had made a decision. I cared too much for Greece to continue to live under military rule as an American. Ironically, the Junta and life under its spies convinced me that rather than continue to be torn between jumping totally into stronger involvement in the opposition or attempting to live a "normal" life as did my Greek in-laws and millions of others (I was married in 1968), I would do better to get on with my life as an American, facing Viet Nam and all the other incredible social changes going on in the States at the time.

When we returned in 1973, it was because we were reading the signs that the end was near. I wanted to be there for the transition and to see if Greece was to be a more permanent home for me.

Once again, public events, political events, set the tone for our private lives. I began teaching again that fall and had settled into enjoying the pleasures and frustrations of Greece and more particularly of Athens. Then the drama at the Polytechnic University next to the National Museum began to build.

What began as a student demonstration for more university rights, similar to student takeovers in the United States and Europe in 1968, quickly became the focus of national protest. In the previous two years the Junta had tried everything possible to keep up its image, its power. Leaders had been rotated, prisoners had been freed, censorship lifted, concessions made. But still protests began to form and mount. And in the fall of 1973 they came to a head at the Polytechneon.

I had just been that evening to see a new musical review written by one of Greece's leading playwrights, Costas Mourselas, aptly entitled *Oh! Dad, What a World!*The whole show satirically attacked much of superficial modern life and even hinted at satire of the dictators. But leaving the theater, we knew immediately that satire had turned to tragic drama. Hundreds of students had barricaded themselves inside the university, painted slogans everywhere, opened a radio station, formed a food brigade as workers and farmers from miles around organized food and supply deliveries to them in sympathy.

We were pushed away by armed police from getting too close. We went home.

But turning on the radio that night, we learned the police had finally attacked, shooting and crushing the students under their small tanks. We listened in angry tears as the student station desperately called out for donors to give blood to the student hospital inside the university. "They are killing us. We are dying." Then the station went dead.

No newspapers carried "complete" coverage, of course.

But over the days and months, the full story began to take shape. Hundreds had been shot, wounded, killed. The total is still not known as far as I know. Several of my students disappeared. And they never showed up again. I never forgot them. I remembered their innocence, their energy, their carefree spirit.

Painfully I was learning once again, not just about Greece and Greeks, but about violence and politics and protest. Would the Junta have fallen eventually without this bloody slaughter? Most likely. But the death of the students in 1973 was a last desperate show of force for a Junta that was doomed.

When the Colonels stepped down (most unusual in the history of dictatorships!) the next summer, Athens was a joyful chaos for days as people danced in the streets, honked horns, set off fireworks, celebrated until they collapsed. As the respected bushy-browed Caramanlis returned from exile in Paris, every announcement of his remarkable effort to move Greece towards democracy again without pushing too far was greeted with enthusiasm and hope.

And the next two years I lived in Greece, 1974-1976, were, for the most part, exhilarating ones in which Greeks returned to a full sense of political life. But democracy is always more work than tyranny. Thus post-Junta Greece was faced with inflation, with the legacy of errors left by the Colonels, and worsening relations with Turkey brought on by the Turkish invasion of Cyprus in 1974, the final event which defeated the Colonels.

I was not living in Greece when Andreas Papandreou came in on a socialist ticket of many popular promises in the 1980s. But my return in 1987 was to a more disgruntled Greece. Perhaps no politician could have delivered all that "Andreas," as he is known, promised. But certainly he had left much unfulfilled, and he had complicated a worsening situation with his own personal scandal (while we were on Kea) by flaunting his affair with a young Olympic airline stewardess (photographed, by the way, dancing in a club on neighboring Kithnos!).

Still, the present disillusioned political spirit in free Greece is preferable to life under the Junta. Yes? Not everyone agrees. During our stay, I became alarmed at how many I met who said, "We need Papadopoulos again." Having seen the entire cycle of life in Greece now from Papadopoulos and his prisons to Papandreou and his promises, I now realize, with less innocence than when I first arrived, how fragile a creature freedom is.

I became friends with Costas Mourselas in the months after the Polytechneon massacre and then translated a number of his short plays into English. But I particularly remember that in the first months of democracy in the fall of 1974 he contributed several scenes to a popular musical review celebrating Greece's return to freedom. In the sketch, two Greek men talk in a cafe-bar about how wonderful it is to be free again and to say whatever they wish. One of the two does exactly that. He shouts anti-government slogans, he makes fun of this politician and that one, and he criticizes various policies taken. The other man remains nervous throughout, constantly looking around and cautioning the other to shut up. "What's wrong with you, old boy?" says the first man. "We have freedom here!" "At this moment we do," says the nervous one, "but when we lose it again others will remember what you said now, and you will be sorry!"

Everyone laughed. But I'm sure most of the audience recognized the truth behind the humor.

I sense this delicate balance that always exists here. History has shown that freedom and tyranny are flip sides of the same coin–rotating, rising and falling. As if to suggest how easily one can slide into the other, while we were on Kea one of Greece's leading comedians, Lazopoulos, was arrested for a night because of his strong satire in his musical review criticizing members of the socialist government! Though he was released the following morning, pressure was put on the army to take him for his service which he had not had to serve up till that point for medical reasons. Such anti-democratic tendencies, once again, herald danger in Greece.

On Kea, however, life has always been less frenzied than in the capital. Kea is on the fringe, not the center. Yes, the island has been occupied, taken, inhabited, influenced by Dorians, Romans, Turks, Germans, Italians, Venetians, and who knows what other groups. But as an agricultural island made up basically of peasant farmers, merchants, and fisherman, Keans have reflected but not suffered the violent upheavals of Athens.

Ironically, the ex-dictator Papadopoulos was kept in a hotel in the harbor of Kea for a week or so after the fall to protect him from angry citizens until his fate could be handled in an orderly fashion. No big deal for Kea. Life went on before, during, and after Papadopoulos here. And it still does.

Communism and Christ

Approaching Kea, the first buildings that are visible are a whitewashed chapel on a cliff and, next to it, a simple whitewashed farmhouse with a bright red hammer and sickle painted across the wall with the letters K K E–the initials of the communist party (or, rather, the largest of several communist parties) in Greece–above the design.

What? A Christian communist island?

No. Just another Greek island and thus a community of people who are, to one degree or another, Orthodox Christians, and who are passionate about politics in all forms, degrees, directions.

The ancient philosophers understood well that man is a political creature. But they would have been more accurate to say, "Greeks are even more political creatures than others!" When I first arrived in Greece years ago, a wise old fellow warned me with a smile, "There are three things you must never argue about with a Greek: religion, football (soccer), and politics."

No truer words were ever spoken. On Kea each of the major parties–the ruling Socialist (PASOK), the Conservative-Moderates (Nea Democratia) and the Communists–had offices. And wherever you went on the island, even in the most remote locations, slogans and party emblems were painted according to party colors: red, of course, for Communists, blue for conservatives, and dark green for the socialists. Furthermore, even for such a small island there were several political rallies staged during our stay, the largest being a Communist gathering with a major party member from Athens speaking.

To my surprise I also saw something during our stay I had never seen before in Greece: They now manufacture small Greek coffee cups (like espresso coffee cups) complete with party emblems. Thus the same shop sells along with its good china and kitchenware, communist, socialist and conservative coffee cups–caffeine and politics!

In 1985, I happened to be in Greece leading a group of New Orleanians at a time that national elections were taking place. Every night, no matter whether we were in Athens or a small village near Delphi, cars paraded around till past midnight honking horns and waving banners and flags as parties alternated evenings for speeches around the country. "It seems more like time for sports rallies than politics," said one of my group. There was such enthusiasm, such "team" devotion, such passion to one's cause. This became even clearer when our socialist bus driver dropped his good-natured attitude and became deadly serious one day when he refused to let a young lady on the bus who happened to be carrying a blue conservative flag. He would not start up the bus with that bloody flag waving behind his back. Period! After much arbitration, I convinced him to drive once the flag had been placed under the bus in the baggage compartment.

To Americans who are used to not exercising their right to vote (we have the lowest voting turnout in the democratic world) such political passion seemed baffling. What does it all mean?

Any answer would be partial. But at root I feel Greeks do care how their village, town, city, country is governed. And each had his or her vision of how things could be better.

I never tired of asking Athenian cab drivers what they think of how things are going. Almost always the remarks begin with, "If I were Prime Minister instead of…," and then they continue nonstop with their excited rendering of a New Republic.

Kea since ancient times has been known for its modesty and balance, and we found this to be true in terms of politics as well. No one party seemed to have the complete monopoly on public affection as in, say, Crete, where the people are eighty percent socialist. And we saw no tempers get far out of control arguing hot issues of the day. In this sense, Kea came to seem to me to be somewhat atypical of Greece. Asked about an issue, an opinion would be given. But the frenzied emotion one finds elsewhere in Greece was, as far as I could detect, absent here.

Yes, the Communist logo welcomed travellers to Kea. But it was, like the many whitewashed chapels themselves, just another part of the pleasing landscape, not a threat or an official flag.

Belonging

Yes, we felt ever more at home on Kea as the days and weeks passed by. We were happy that we not only recognized most folk in town but they acknowledged us as well, especially Sam, who had become a kind of unofficial Hora mascot.

But it was in mid October that I felt we belonged. Argiris would pull up a chair and talk to us about his youth in the countryside of Kea, and Yannis would not only hug Sam every time he saw him, but also felt easy enough about us that he could sit at his desk in the shop and pluck long hairs from his nose in front of a small mirror propped up on an evaporated milk can.

What really convinced me we belonged, however, was the October morning at the kafeneon that Angelos, one of the taxi drivers, bought me a Greek coffee. I smiled all morning.

Second Encounter with Dionysios

The second time I ran into Dionysios, we were attending a performance of Aristophanes' *Peace* in Athens under a moonlit September sky in the ancient theater of Herodes Attikos. I have a particular fondness of comedy and for Aristophanes especially, so we had left Kea in order to see what a modern production of this ancient comedy would be like.

Imagine my surprise, once again, when I spotted Dionysios, seated on the cushioned stone seats just behind us, with a beautiful Swedish woman on one arm and an enchanting Greek woman on the other. He, in fact, saw me first.

"How's Kea?"

"Oh! It's you again…fine…the tourists have left," I replied. "But I thought you were headed for America."

"Soon," he smiled. "But while the weather is so pleasant here…."

The theater was filling up as dark descended. Three or four thousand people, more Greek than foreign, but still a fair number of tourists from everywhere including bus loads from Japan, were taking their seats.

Dionysios had snuck a bottle of wine into the theater and offered me some after taking a generous pull at the bottle himself.

"Do you usually attend ancient dramas?" I asked, feeling awkward, "I mean, I know you are the god of drama but…."

He laughed and gave the Swedish beauty a kiss.

"I don't bother with the tragedies anymore. The modern Greeks do them badly. Too stiff, too serious, too…stuffy! Not like the old days. But comedy…. That's a different matter. I never miss Aristophanes," and he pointed to the full theater. "And the Greeks love him too! If this were a tragedy, the theater might be half empty!"

"How do you explain this!"

"Very simple. Greeks have a better sense of humor than a sense of tragedy. They tend to laugh at faults and foibles and troubles rather than cry. How do you feel?"

"I quite agree," I said. "But from what I can see, our American sense of the comic isn't as developed or as deep as the Greek."

This caught Dionysios' attention. He took his arm from around the Greek woman and leaned forward.

"What do you mean? What about Woody Allen and Buster Keaton and…"

"They are great. But even Woody Allen isn't able to work at the same scope and depth as Aristophanes."

Dionysios laughed.

"You're right, my friend," he said. "You know what Aristophanes called himself? Komodidaskalos...."

"A teacher-through-comedy," I added.

"Bravo," Dionysios exclaimed. "You see. We take comedy seriously. Comedy is fun and can be very silly too, but it also can have something to teach us. Aristophanes is loved because he did all of these things. So...I'm proud to be the god of comedy and drama. Like wine, you see, comedy and tragedy take you outside yourself, both to forget small troubles and to get a fresh perspective on what's what. Understand?"

"It makes sense!"

"Exactly. That's why we put political cartoons on the front page of newspapers instead of buried inside like you Americans. And what about our famous hero of shadow puppet theater, Karangyosis. He is comic too, but he is much more than that; he represents the Greek people, struggling, half clever, half stupid, but a survivor!"

"You have a point."

"Of course!" and he took another sip of wine.

"You will learn in the United States," I said, "that America is still not ready for Aristophanes. No one dares to perform him as he was most likely performed in ancient times, complete with artificial phalluses and ribald behavior, especially buggering. And I've even had parents complain when I teach Aristophanes in class."

Dionysios laughed.

"A country that produced W.C. Fields can't be all bad," he said. "And what about Groucho! He cracks me up every time!"

The lights began to dim and music started up.

Dionysios whispered quickly.

"You are right, my friend. Our comedy and humor is very different from American. And I think the basic difference is this...not just that you are a puritan nation which began without any humor and so have had to rush to catch up...not just that...but a basic difference is that Aristophanes built on folk humor, laughter of the people, that is a festive, liberating, life-giving sense of humor that embraces the whole of human experience, the sexual, the scatological, the lyrical, the tragic even. And to this, Aristophanes added something else-fantasy. Most of your American comedy is romantic comedy...boy meets girl stuff...even Chaplin is that way...and Woody Allen. But Aristophanes is very Greek because romance was never a part of our heritage. That's your Western Middle Ages invention. For Aristophanes, comedy meant that a character has a crazy idea that he or she carried out by himself/herself and succeeds: the total individual. And then this success, this triumph is celebrated. Festivity and fantasy...in a balance that has never been seen again in the world, not even in the Marx Brothers whom I love so much, though they come close."

I nodded. Dionysios patted me on the shoulder and *Peace* began.

As the play unfolded, I thought about what Dionysios had said. Clearly he was right. The "seriousness" of *Peace* was apparent. A farmer was sick and tired of war (Aristophanes was writing during the Peloponnesian War which ultimately destroyed Athenian democracy) and flies to Zeus on a dung-eating beetle to conclude a separate peace treaty with the king of gods himself. And does so. The second half of the play is simply a glorious, wide-open celebration of peace which includes the first expression of group sex in Western literature (all the farmers are invited by Trygaius, the farmer, to "enjoy" Peace, personified as a beautiful goddess in the play).

I thought of the old cook throwing bones in the sea.

I remembered Zorba laughing when all his and his boss' plans for a revamped mine ended in disaster, and Zorba's response was to laugh, to call the disaster a "beautiful catastrophe" and to dance, dance, dance.

Recent Greek cartoons in the newspapers also came to mind. One by the great cartoonist Kyr, for instance, showed a backdrop of a very sterile, ugly, polluted Athens as a mugger with a gun holds up a citizen saying "Your money or your life." And the frustrated citizen replies, "What money? What life?"

And I chuckled to myself to remember how often Argiris and Vasso would turn misfortune into laughter, especially Vasso, her large frame shaking with laughter.

Yes, for the Greeks, I sensed, humor and comedy is a way of perceiving life. It is both knowledge and therapy. Again I am reminded of Aristotle's remark that a person is not a human being until age forty days or so when he or she first laughs. In other words, to laugh is to be human.

With a laughter that cuts much deeper than American humor. I thought about how the recent revelation that the prime minister, Andreas Papandreou, had a young mistress had not destroyed his political career or marriage as it had brought ruin and hardship to American politicians, most visibly presidential candidate Gary Hart. In fact, the Greeks loved all of the jokes about Andreas that had suddenly sprung up. One comedian, already popular, became even more in the limelight with his Aristophanic-like quips about the affair. Harry Klein, the comedian, made the nation laugh as he pretends to quote Mrs. Papandreou on learning of her seventy-year-old husband's affair: "I know who he does it with, I know where he does it, but I don't know with what he does it!"–humor and politics going together once again as they always have in Greece since ancient times.

But this production of *Peace* was very different. Directed by the innovative and controversial director Spyros Evangelatos, this version was closer to Brecht's theater of alienation than to Aristophanes' joyful fantasies. The program notes explain that the setting was "some time after World War III" when a troupe of actors happen upon the costumes for Aristophanes' *Peace*. The whole production, therefore, had a troubling double edge to it which kept us from enjoying the more carefree energy that Aristophanes had built into his script and which I had seen in other productions of the play.

A sense of doom and disaster hung over the set even though some parts were still uproariously funny.

The ending was quite unexpected, however,

In Aristophanes' text, the play concludes with a joyous festival of carnivalesque laughter, drinking, dancing, sexuality, celebration. Evangelatos provided a more muted celebration around the goddess "Peace," played by a real actress lodged in a huge "statue." But the play did not stop here. As the celebration quieted down, the goddess suddenly dislodges herself from her base and eerily flees from the stage, her white robes trailing, leaving the statue of Peace…empty as the actors reach out in vain to her departing image.

This ending was chillingly contemporary and disquieting to say the least. The hearty laughter of Aristophanes, Evangelatos seemed to suggest, is not possible in today's world, even in Greece.

It was an impressive interpretation of the comic poet, but a disturbing one.

So I turned to discuss it with Dionysios, only to find that he too had disappeared…with the Swede. Only the Greek beauty remained. And an empty bottle.

She saw my distressed glance and smiled and shrugged her shoulders.

"Like Peace, Dionysios comes and goes," she laughed ironically. "What can I say. What can we do!"

Her laughter, however, had said enough.

The Metalsmith

Over time, we visited various workshops in Hora. There was one woodworking shop, for instance, where Sam delighted in picking up scraps of wood on the floor and watching the old fellow and his young assistant shape a door frame or build a cabinet.

But we did not get to see the metalsmith in action until late September when we were returning from one of our hikes.

We seldom walked the upper part of the village away from our house. So when we saw the door open as we passed, we looked in. A hot oak fire was burning and the shop's owner was busy heating a plough blade in the flame as his assistant, a man also in his sixties, operated the largest pair of bellows I've seen, roughly four feet in height.

The metalsmith motioned us in.

Sam didn't know what to make of all of this. He was mesmerized by the flame, the reddened metal blade, the "master" who shaped the blade even thinner and then dunked it steaming into a nearby pot of water. Meanwhile, the bellows operator, "the windmaker" (fisayros), kept up a steady pumping rhythm.

Just a typical day in a metalworking shop in a village, but totally unique for us modern city folk who had never seen anything like it before…or since.

Byzantines and Turks

We never ran out of chapels for Sam to carry out his candle lighting pleasure.

Roughly 400 chapels and churches for 1800 people? What does this say about Keans? What does this say about their attitudes toward religion, and toward family since most of these are family chapels? And how does one relate this to Athens, where one certainly doesn't find a chapel for every four-and-a-half people?

To begin to suggest dimensions and ways of answering these questions is to speak of the nature of life during the Byzantine Empire–a span of approximately a thousand years–and under Turkish domination–some four hundred years. While a number of important studies of Greek village life have been written from anthropological and sociological perspectives, none that I have come across does justice to these twin molding influences on the Greek character.

In the past, I have led three tours to Greece for my university, and I am always pleased when a trip ends and my fellow travellers have at least come to appreciate that Greece is an area with a lot more history than just the Classical period of 5th-century Athens. The vast history of Greece before the Classical period has only been hinted at here: the Minoans, Myceneans, Cycladic cultures, and earlier Bronze Age and Neolithic. But part of what Antonis Samarakis suggests in his "Greece has no culture" remarks is that Greece has had many cultures and therefore is an extremely complicated patchwork of influences.

"At no time in history does there appear to have existed a pure Greek race," writes George Theotokas, one of the major figures in modern Greek literature between the Wars–an important observation, missed by experts and laymen alike. To those I've taken around Greece who expect to see a pure race of noble profiled Greeks, each looking like the Charioteer of Delphi or Venus de Milo, I mention Theotokas. The people who have lived here have been short and dark and tall and blond. They have been Mediterraneans and Northerners such as the Dorians. They have been Turks and Arabs and Italians and French and Slavs and Spanish Jews and even, after World War II, German-Greeks–and everything in between. No pure master Greek race. Period.

But there was a Byzantine Empire, and that has left its traces in many more ways than the Classical world of Pericles. What has puzzled the West for hundreds of years has been the huge contradiction of Byzantium. It was the first Empire dedicated to a Christian God. And yet it was one of the bloodiest of empires if judged by wars, palace intrigues, and civil strife within its own shifting borders.

The contradiction is real, but to focus only on this aspect of Byzantium is to miss the point of the longest lasting empire in history. Western Europe during this period–roughly 400 A.D. to 1453–developed as a territory of separate countries and kingdoms organized on feudal systems. In Byzantium, all territory was one empire under God. Beyond that level, the family emerged as the strongest unit, quite unlike the feudal development of Europe. God and family were the twin poles of a thousand years of rule, and still are, in many ways, the orientation of modern Greeks.

Everything else–the aristocracy, the military, the merchant class, the slaves–fit in somewhere between. Space does not allow, of course, for a full explanation, nor am I qualified to give the topic its due. But certainly one reason the Byzantine period lasted so long, despite constant attacks from all sides by Turks, Arabs and others, was because that as long as both God and family could be upheld, flexible arrangements could be worked out to solve all other problems. For example, the Byzantines allowed people to worship God in their own language. This flexibility won the empire many converts that the Latin Church of Rome lost in its dogmatic insistence on worship in Latin. Another example is that Orthodox priests were allowed to marry. Thus to this day, one of the attractive features of the Orthodox faith is that a priest can truly be a full member of his community (no female priests yet, but can the day be far off?).

One empire under God. And as such, the Byzantines passed down some of the most beautiful artwork—mosaics, frescoes, ikons—and architecture—St. Sophia and many other churches and monasteries that we have. Also in the name of the Christian God, Byzantine scholars preserved the glories of the ancient past. Without their preservation of the Alexandrian library (much of course was still lost), the Renaissance in Europe would not have been possible in the form and dimension it took.

The ancient Greeks were centered, during the peak of their culture in the 5th century B.C. on civic activity, thus no palaces, no splendid homes, no elaborate private temples. The Parthenon is the building for all Athens.

Not so under the Byzantine period. Of course Constantinople was the City and Saint Sophia was the center of the Orthodox faith. But with such a strong emphasis on family, it was only natural that what we still see on Kea should have developed: family churches, a family's direct link with the spiritual. This fact also reflects the loose arrangement the Orthodox church has with its members. Unlike American churches, say, where one is expected to attend regularly and participate in a variety of extra-religious activities such as bake sales, building funds and "retreats," those of the Orthodox faith are much less regulated. There are the main feast days and holidays to celebrate and the major transitions of baptism, marriage and death. But in between, regular attendance and organized activities have never been part of the package. They are Christians. What is the need to be in a specific building at a specific time? This explains the poor attendance at regular Masses and the locked doors on so many of the chapels we tried with Sam to enter and light a ten drachma candle. If it's a family chapel, there is no need to leave it open to the public. Of course, others have the opposite feeling: it's our church but it should be available to all. Take your pick! Nobody has told them how it should be.

The importance of the family needs less comment because it is so apparent, particularly outside of Athens. How many homes have we entered to find the grandmother in black sitting there with the youngest of children while the mother is out shopping and the father is at work in the countryside. Life was never easy under the Byzantine period and, it was a lot worse under the Turks. So family was what one had to rely on to get on in the world or just to survive. There is, for instance, a fascinating body of commentaries from the era warning people to be suspicious of anyone who was not a family member. Who could you trust!

These twin influences—God and family—became even more critical during the four hundred years of Turkish domination. The Church played a heroic role in keeping alive not only religion, but the language, the literature, the culture.

The many "secret schools" established by priests throughout Greece during the Ottoman period assured the survival of a Hellenic spirit. And the close-knit interdependency of members within each family also guaranteed that despite murders, rapes, kidnappings, and economic hardships, "Greeks" would be.

But more must be said about the Turkish era. While much of the Hellenic culture made it through to 1826 and the War of Greek Independence, the Greeks nevertheless absorbed a lot of Turkish culture as well. Take the food and the coffee, for instance. Remove the Middle Eastern influence and not much remains. Greek coffee is Turkish coffee, no doubt about it, and souflaki is shiskabob, and so on. Yet, as always, the Greeks have made these influences their own: a bit of this spice here, a variation in cooking there.

The same is true of language. There have been estimates that modern Greek has as much as a twenty percent loan base vocabulary from Turkish. Again, though many Greeks I've spoken with are upset by such a revelation, this is to be expected. How can you live with another culture side by side and often closer than that and not pick up many of their expressions, recipes, habits.

"Our real virtue as modern Greeks is this," a leading Greek sculptress once told me, "that no matter how many times we have been conquered, we've never been completely defeated. And no matter how many foreign influences pour in, we always turn them into something else, something that is ours, finally!"

She didn't have to search far for examples. "Take our beloved Shadow Theater Hero, Karangyosis! Even his name is Turkish: Karagyoz means `Dark Eyes' in Turkish. Yet by the mid-nineteenth century, he was a Greek peasant clever enough to defeat the most powerful Turk by using his mind!"

She laughed. And I couldn't help but think that beyond God and family, laughter has helped Greeks to be survivors too.

When Festivity Holds Sway

It was the evening of October 27th, the day before a major Greek holiday, "Oxi" Day ("No" Day), the celebration of the Greek defeat of the Italians in 1940. On Kea, there was definitely a festive spirit in the cold mountain air.

Just as we were headed down to Argiris' to eat, Greek resistance songs poured out across the village from the platea. We hurried down to find some school children helping to bring in large boughs of daphi (bay leaves!) to make wreaths for the following morning's ceremonies. Loudspeakers were set on the town hall balcony, and the music played as those in the "city government" worked to get ready for the festivities. Yorghos, the mayor, was there tying up the daphi and even sweeping up afterwards.

After supper we hear another kind of music: bouzouki music, the popular music of modern Greece.

It didn't take long to figure out where it was coming from: packed into the small office of the Civilizing Club of Kea was a local bouzouki player, an electric base guitar player, the assistant mayor singing with the microphone almost inside his mouth–as is the custom in bouzouki clubs everywhere–and the mayor on tambourine. A few young fellows were also inside enjoying this unusual concert. Both instruments were electrified and put out a lot of noise across the town that usually remains silent.

We soon got caught up in the music. It was surprisingly professional! Once warmed up, the assistant mayor, Dimitri, swung into a hot rendition of a tried and true classic by the late king of bouzouki, Tsitsanis: "Cloudy Sunday" ("Synifiasmeni Kyriaki"). They were damned good, as good as most of the unknown small groups on Bourbon Street in New Orleans, blaring out to the shifting masses milling back and forth carrying sixteen-ounce beer cups or deadly hurricane drinks. But there on Kea the music was in the Civilizing Club instead of a night club, and there was not a drink in sight, not even a 7-Up or cola. Just music…and on the shelves, beneath the paintings by local artists, photos from previous festive occasions of dancers and musicians.

I was inside when Odette signalled for me to come out. There in the dark and cold of the main street, arms raised, Sam was hopping around in his own version of a Zorba type syrtaki solo dance. Sam caught the musicians' attention too, and they began to play to and for Sam who danced and danced and danced, whirling in ever more energetic circles.

The celebration had begun.

The official part was held the following morning in the platea at 10:30.

There were probably an equal number of people gathered in this one spot during the August 15th Feast of the Virgin, but many of them would have been relatives and friends from Athens. The 28th of October Festivities, therefore, brought together the largest number of Keans we had seen.

Several hundred townsfolk ringed the square, which has a war memorial in the center dedicated not only to the World Wars but to the Balkan War of 1912-1913, and to the Turkish conflict of the 1920s. All of the school children, from kindergarten through high school, marched into the square behind Greek blue and white flags and two drums played by young village girls. All were dressed in blue sweaters, white shirts/blouses and grey slacks/skirts. A few of the youngest kids were dolled up in traditional outfits. This meant the impressive evzone "fustinella" white skirt for the boy, the costume of the mountain men of Northern Greece who fought in the War of Independence, and a full embroidered dress for the little girl with a red fez-like cap and tassel. Across from them were the Kean officials: the mayor, the three priests, the police, and some military figure. Up above and behind were some older fellows, who were no longer in school (only elementary school is compulsory), and old men.

Cold, bright sunlight.

Speeches were given from the mayor's balcony in the town hall. The longest speech was given by the young school teacher from Cyprus, a fellow who truly looked like an effective teacher and spoke directly and with sincerity to the whole assembly. He was followed by school children beginning with the kindergarten kids, who had memorized short verses. The smallest kids were sweet, funny, and drew applause from everyone. They all lay wreaths at the base of the war memorial. And I couldn't help but think how much more I would enjoy this kind of celebration–little kids scrubbed and shined struggling but happy to deliver their lines about freedom–if I were a Greek veteran, than I would viewing the annual military parade in Athens.

Then came the dancing by two groups of high school girls–each of ten, and both very good–all doing the dance that has been the basic step throughout the Mediterranean Middle East and Balkans for thousands of years: the group circle, line dance, a dance based on being joined to those beside you in one ever-moving line, a joyful celebration of union and community, and a dance which also allows for individuality as the line is broken for some steps and each does her own turns, twirls. They were beautiful. And their dancing in the bright chilly sun of October transcended the badly amplified taped music. All watched with awe, interest, pride, lust, even love.

There was no official feast afterwards. But the square filled quickly with locals and with others I recognized as "costal" folk from the villages along the coast. Good cheer reigned. "I don't usually like the loud volume of conversation in a taverna in Greece," Odette observed, "but this is just right for today and somehow the noise warms up the place too."

Over wine and food that day I thought about all the festive times on Kea and the other islands. And I remembered what Homer tells us are the best times of our lives. The words are those of Odysseus speaking at a feast given in his honor, as a Stranger, before his identity is known:

"For I think there is no occasion accomplished that is more pleasant
than when festivity holds sway among all the populace,

and the feasters up and down the houses are sitting in order
and listening to the singer, and beside them the tables are loaded
with bread and meats, and from the mixing bowl the wine steward
draws the wine and carries it about and fills the cups.
This seems to my own mind to be the best of occasions."
We toasted Odysseus and ordered another bottle.

Owls

"I've been asked," Lou told me one day, "why I finally decided to buy a house in Hora."

"Why did you?" I ask.

"Because of the owls," he said with a smile.

I had to think about that one.

But it didn't take long. Not only is it difficult for one living in an urban area to understand how peaceful and silent a village without traffic can be, but until you do live away from mechanical noise, it is impossible for the ear to begin to distinguish between the different natural sounds.

After Lou mentioned the Kean owls–a small, compact-sized form of the species–I listened for them. And there they were, punctuating the cool evenings with their soothing cooing, which sounded halfway between a purr and a hum. We seldom saw them,. but the owls were there, in numbers I had not experienced anywhere else.

Namedays

Greeks celebrate namedays rather than birthdays, that is, their saint's day, since Greeks are names after religious figures, famous and obscure. There's something infinitely sane about this. After all, by placing the emphasis on a name rather than a date, it is continuity and unity and similarity ("I belong to a long tradition of Dimitris") that is feted, not aging.

October 26th is St. Dimitrios Day. And Kea, in its reserved way, was all aflutter. Dimitri is like David in English. It seems like one in three Greek men are Dimitris. And the same is almost true for women with the feminine form: Dimitria.

The day had particular meaning to us since we live a stone's throw from the second largest church in Hora, St. Dimitrios. This huge, ugly, rectangular "unGreek"-styled church put up in 1898 in Kea's heyday had always been locked up every time Sam and I would go up to it so he could ride his tricycle around the tiled yard...except for a wedding a few weeks before on a chilly Sunday.

But beginning the night before–October 25th–bells rang, lights were strung in the courtyard, flags were flown, and Masses chanted.

By 10:00 a.m. on the 26th, half the village seemed to be inside the church. All the school children in their new jogging suits (the fashion this year) were there, as well as mothers with babies, old fellows I'd never seen on canes, thin young men I'd also never seen before in suits, and a bevy of priests and alter boys, chanting, shaking incense, all illuminated by a sunburst of light inside reflected off the bright brass fixtures and ornaments. And mountains of fresh cut bread at the entrance, which was passed out to one and all.

We called our friend Dimitri, the TV director, in Athens to wish him kronia pola" (many years), and wished the same to Dimitri the cab driver to and from the beach, which, even so late in the season, still had its attractive days.

And I remembered my first two years of teaching in Greece, at Athens College. I taught ninth grade, and I was surprised and interested the first time that first year that one of my young fellows showed up in class with a box of sweets and asked for time out from English to pass them out since it was his "name day." No problem. I was pleased to oblige. But then I realized some weeks later and many rich, thick sweets later, that I had opened a floodgate of namedays. Though St. Dimitrios day is practically a national holiday, there are, of course, name days every week for somebody, including a kind of "All Saints Day" for insignificant saints and those with no official saints. Thus I was forced to amend my American generosity and become the stern old teacher who required sweets to be passed out at the end of the lesson.

I saw one old man with a cane hobbling down a steep lane later during the day. People were wishing him happy nameday. So when I drew close, so did I, also adding, "How are you?"

"I'm still walking," he returned, "still walking."

And on Kea, where nothing but donkeys and people can pass through the streets, I realized that as long as you can walk, there is hope of another nameday to come.

Departed Friends

Not all bones I thought about on Kea were in the sea. Many were friends I had known over the years in Greece who were no more. Death had taken away more than I at first had remembered, and the reality of such absence caused me to be silent from time to time on a walk or sitting by the sea or falling asleep at night. Gone was Harry, nicknamed The Snowman, who had been a pilot and a hero in the Greek Air Force in World War II and who loved the classics, told great stories, drank too much, and who spent his spare time putting together several excellent Greek-English dictionaries. Gone was Platon, the most gentle and good-humored and "civilized" man I have known, a lover of life and drama and satire who devoted his time to education and theater, both as a translator and promoter of good drama for more than fifty years. Gone was Jason, a bright and troubled philosopher who after the collapse of the promise of the 1960s held that the best life was the uninvolved life and that the best "uninvolvement" of all was suicide, an act he carried out thus proving himself a true philosopher or a desperate human being. Gone, too, other teaching colleagues and some students, and relatives of good friends, such as Costa, my playwright friend's wife. But while these losses saddened me, they did not depress me. For there is something in the way most Greeks live their lives that makes death less a tragedy than a part of a larger cycle of existence.

I thought about how Antonis Samarakis, my friend the writer, captures such a triumphant attitude in one of his short stories, "The Last Participation," which I have translated. It concerns a funeral for a "father" which is attended by the whole family, including the young son who is imprisoned by the dictatorship police for protesting tyranny and who is let out in handcuffs for an hour to pay his respects. As the story concludes we finally realize that it has been narrated by the corpse, the father, from his coffin as it is about to be lowered into the earth. The father concludes the tale thusly:

"My Eleni was ready to throw the red rose into the still open coffin when at the same moment the three escorts closed in on Dimitri and started to pull him away and my Eleni turned and ran after him and placed the red rose in Dimitri's handcuffed hands as they pushed him on and he left us and a third drop of rain landed on my moustache and as the coffin descended down and down I felt a last desire for life. I felt the agony and hope of all, it was my last participation in life and in my eyes burns the solitary red rose which they had rightfully placed in Dimitri's temporarily bound hands rather than in my own permanently bound hands which I feel growing colder and colder as I descend further into the earth and depart, depart...."

Not even Death can keep a Greek from telling one last tale, from having one last participation in life. My friends were much the same and continue to live in my memory.

Kyria Vasso's Foolproof Lentils

I happen to love lentil soup. I cook it every winter at least once a week and never the same way twice. Imagine my pleasure one cold evening in late October when Kyria Vasso got around to formalizing the arrival of winter by putting on a steaming pot of lentils.

They were incomparable. And extremely simple to brew.

According to Vasso, this is all you need do:

"One bag of large bean lentils. They heat up much faster than
    the small ones.

"Five toes of garlic.

"Two large onions.

"A small can of tomato paste.

"Two bay leaves.

"Cook for an hour and add salt to taste five minutes before the end."

The Louisiana variation is also simple. Double the garlic and onions, and dash generously with cayenne pepper.

Strikes and Blues

Our last month was ushered in with labor strikes and some fine Mississippi Delta blues.

In New Orleans, we rent out the other half of our creole cottage to Jon, a thirty-year-old playwright-bluesman. In the past two years Jon has teamed up with some of the best of the old-time black blues singers, acted as a kind of manager too, and traveled the States and Europe singing the blues.

Through friends in Greece and some support from the American Embassy, a one-night performance was finally arranged for Jon and Eddie "Guitar" Burns in an Athenian club.

Having Jon as a tenant has been, for us, part of what living in New Orleans is all about. For the past year or so before Jon joined forces with Eddie Burns, he played with another blues agent, R.L. Burnside. "Rule," as he is known, is sixty, the father of sixteen, a boozer, and one hell of a blues player. But because he is always poor (no plumbing or electricity in his Mississippi country home), he stayed with Jon on his side of our house whenever he was in New Orleans. So we experiences many days and nights of hearing R.L. and Jon jamming next door, and numerous times when Sam would sit in R.L.'s lap, happily silent and apparently mesmerized by this gentle man with huge hands and a tough but quiet voice.

We didn't want to miss the chance to see Jon, the blues and Athens come together. Only something so worthwhile could now get us off of Kea, but this was more than a reason to make the journey. We called all our friends and went.

Athens is, as I have said, a city of death, becoming worse by the day. But I have, of course, had good times there and have old friends and new living in this modern catastrophe. Thus, I wanted to write some glowing words about Athens during Easter–when the whole city is empty as everyone heads for his or her village to celebrate and those lucky ones who remain are able to walk freely in clear air without being run over–or to describe some of the hidden nooks and crannies of the city where fine little coffee shops and tavernas have miraculously managed to survive, or to talk about an Athens which used to have a building code downtown restricting buildings to six floors maximum in order to preserve a view of the Acropolis from any location. It would only be fair to balance my harsh words, after all.

But our early November return wiped out any such intentions. The pollution, traffic, unfriendly pushing, shoving bodies, I could handle. Normal. No serious problem for a three-day visitor who adopts a certain Zen-like distance and perspective on it all. Yet to take on everyday Athens and a three-day coordinated strike, which included banks, post offices, telephone companies, and schools, was too much.

The morning after our arrival back to Dimitri and Katerina's house, I rushed down to the bank to withdraw drachmas on my credit card. "Sorry, we are on strike."

But there was a long line of customers who were being served, slowly to be sure, by the managers who were on duty. If they were being helped, why not I? "We cannot handle credit cards, but we can handle other things," was the answer from a well-fed, well-clothed little manager. He suggested I try a branch office. "Maybe someone there can help you."

I tried the office he suggested. And eight other banks during the next three hours. I explained that I had not a drachma on me (true) and that there must be some way for somebody to do something. Years of living in Greece had taught me to be Greek to the degree of never taking "no" as a final word. Thus the importance of "connections" (ta mesa). And of dramatics. And persistence. I had no connections, so I settled down to applying the other two "rules of the game." For no matter how difficult things had been during the five years I had lived here before, there had always been a way.

But this time, now, no luck. Every bank referred me back to my starting point, the central office. I came back to the same well-fed little manager. "No luck," I told him. He shrugged. "There must be something you can do," I said. "I have no money and a child who has to eat for the next three days. The strike is one thing, eating another. Surely you could handle this yourself." "It's impossible," he said. "But my hungry child?" (dramatics and persistence). "Have patience," he said. "Can a baby live on patience?" (melodrama and anger). I stormed out.

Of course I was personally angry. But I could solve my immediate problem by depending on the kindness of friends. But that was not the point. I sensed strongly now, more clearly than before, that a whole attitude was changing, had changed in Greece. Modern Greece, for better or worse, has been constructed for the most part as an effort by millions in free enterprise: individuals setting up their tavernas, their fleets of ships, their import-export shops, their coffee shops and small farms. But all of that has changed. The family business is caving in to multinational corporations, and private initiative is evolving into the lack of initiative created by those who are on the public payroll. A recent survey of young Greeks reveals that something like seventy percent want to work for some form of civil service so as to punch a clock, get a monthly salary (and an extra month's check at Christmas and Easter), take regular holidays, fade into retirement at an agreed upon age. No risks, no thrills, no spills.

The result of such a change in national attitude has been a low productivity rate in economic terms–the Greeks are increasingly aware that they will never be truly competitive in the common market in the near or even far future–and a "I don't give a damn" impersonal mentality at the personal level.

With "have patience" still ringing in my ears, I tried to carry out other errands. But the post office was also on strike as was the telephone office, and on my way to and fro to these various offices, I kept running into hundreds of students waving banners on a three-day strike of their own protesting Greek education. ("Bravo," said one of the taxi drivers when we returned to Kea. "Greek education should be blown up!")

I was definitely becoming frustrated, angry, blue.

Thus all the more fortunate that Jon and Eddie Burns showed up at Ah! Maria!–a club frequented by many young folk–to play the blues.

A Monday night in Athens? I wasn't expecting much. And knowing that Greeks come late, I expected the 9:30 show to get under way at 10:00. But by 9:15 almost all of the five hundred seats around the small tables were taken. Then Jon and Eddie came on stage, Jon on harmonica and Eddie on steel guitar, and they wailed for two hours and several encores.

The crowd loved them. About a hundred more were turned away at the door. Odette, myself, and our friends, Dimitri and Katerina, drank whiskey from the bottle we smuggled in as a tribute to the evening and we felt very good indeed.

"My baby is nineteen, and I just can't keep that woman satisfied," sang sixty-year-old Eddie, the father of six legitimate children and many others he claims are here and there. The crowd applauded. "I ask her where she's goin' and she just tells me where she's been," he goes on. The audience is clapping along. Jon hits intricate notes and rhythms on his harmonica, and whoever was operating lights tried too hard to mix up the spots and blues and reds and soft whites.

But it didn't matter. On a bitter cold winter night in Athens five hundred Greeks were thrilled to hear what they have heard too little of: the real blues.

Somehow the blues and the Greek young folk helped to make the troubles of the day fade away. The blues can do that. And, as strange as it might sound at first, the Greeks understand that. They have, after all, their own version of the blues: the rhembetiko music from the bars and drug centers of Asia Minor in the 1920s when several million Greeks from that region resettled in Greece and brought their music and traditions with them. In fact, as originally planned, the evening was to feature Jon and Eddie, then some rhembetes, some of the old Greek players, that is, then a joint gig of both groups jamming. It did not happen and might have been something of a mess if it had. But the similarity was not lost on the eager young Greeks in Ah! Maria!

Sam was with us, partially because we had our usual problem–no baby-sitter–but also because Jon is his friend too, and because in New Orleans, for such good music, bringing children along is part of growing up in the City That Care Forgot.

We felt a streak of homesickness. The show helped us realize that as much as we were enjoying Kea, we only had a month to go. We felt torn.

"I'm gonna bring it all back home!" sang Eddie. And so will we, all too soon.

Strangers, Tourists and Travellers

Xenos is the Greek word for both stranger and foreigner. But it means more. A xenos is someone "not from here," thus unknown, and as such, since Homeric times, held to be worthy of respect. Remember that Odysseus was wined and dined in various palaces on his way home from Troy even before he told his hosts who he was. The point was that strangers are protected by the gods and should thus be cared for. In Euripides' play, *Children of Heracles,* there is no question that Heracles' children will be protected by the Athenians with whom they ask refuge as strangers condemned to death by Argos because, "Stranger, respect is due suppliants of the gods."

As a student reading Homer, I always marvelled over such a concept of hospitality to strangers. Of course any second thought about the matter, convinces one of the complete sanity of such a custom. Homer was describing a time of great uncertainty when kings often became slaves or exiles and the wheel of fortune could and did turn swiftly. Thus treating others as you would like to be treated yourself should you come asking for help made a lot of sense. But I didn't expect the custom to have survived down through the ages.

However, often during my first few years in Greece, visiting in the most out-of-the-way places, I would be invited into a home, especially in the countryside, sit down, and be treated to a small tray with a candied fruit, a coffee, and ouzo and a glass of water. On my visit to the Holy Mountain, Mt. Athos, in 1975, each monastery carried philoxenia–hospitality to strangers–out to a combined Greek-Christian extreme. We were given free room and board at each monastery along with the traditional sweet, ouzo and coffee when just passing through.

But, once again, times have changed.

Things aren't as they once were. Tourism has changed most of such a concept of hospitality, along with many other aspects of Greek culture. And while Greeks often lump tourists in as xenoi, more often they are particular to keep touristes and xenoi separate. For years tourism has been the major industry of Greece. It has made the careers of many, and turned millions into part of the service industry chain, from gift shop operators to those villagers who rent donkeys or bicycles for the hour.

The change in attitude is complicated and often subtle. It has meant, of course, that many are out for a fast buck and cut corners any way they can to take advantage of those who come from abroad, or even from other parts of Greece, if they can get away with it. Each time I return to Greece, sad to say, I run into more incidents of being cheated than the visit before.

And on Kea too. No problem with Hora, for few tourists stay here: there is one pension that doubles as a shoe shop and the small Hotel Ioulis with its "magnificent sunsets." But down along the coast in the fishing village of Vourkari, a different breed of Keans have developed. Vourkari is a regular stopping point for many yachts, big and small. So the tavernas and shops along the harbor cater to these German and British and French upwardly mobile folk.

In late October we took advantage of a warm day, jumped in the sea at our old beach, Yialoskari, and did what we had never done during our stay: headed over to Vourkari for lunch. What the hell–a change of pace, a chance to try out another place.

Only one taverna was open, run by a dour-faced oldish fellow and a non-communicative young waiter. The three tables of touristes were all German yacht people. They were knocking back the wine and beer, untroubled by the poor food, bad service and inflated prices. And there you have the catch. Many tourists don't expect much, are willing to pay the price and so get exactly that.

But we expected more, not only because we were living in Greece and so saw ourselves as xenoi rather than as touristes, but also because we spoke Greek. At Vourkari this all meant nothing. Even though we had a young child, a table of yachters got served before us, and the waiter was more than half an hour in finally reaching us. If that were the only sin committed, I might have forgotten the incident. More was to follow, however.

I had ordered a small bottle of retsina wine (40 cents). The vacant-eyed waiter brought me an open bottle of dry white wine (3 dollars): "I wanted retsina." "We are out of it," he quipped, with not a trace of an excuse. Smoke began to rise from our ears.

Then Odette cut into her grilled cutlets, two pieces on the plate and one of them nothing but bone and fat. There literally was no meat to be found. She was up immediately thrusting it into the dour owner's face. Beyond all belief, he tried to point out some meat to her. When she retaliated showing him there was none, he shrugged his shoulders and went back to his grill. This was too much. We did not want grilled meat anyway and only took it because the menu had two choices, both double the price of Argiris'.

Of course when we left we deducted the price of the meat from the bill. And I found myself using on this fellow some of the stronger Greek curses that would make a bishop blush. It took us several hours to calm down, not just for this one event, but for the increasing attitude in Greece and other tourist-oriented countries that the tourist is a foreigner to be used rather than respected.

This "tourist mentality" extends even to the police. Odette found several times that the Kea police would speed by in their black and white jeep shouting out to her as she walked with Sam, wearing ordinary clothing. And at the same taverna meal just described, we listened to a German resident of Kea for the past five years who had just been given a stiff fine for driving without her license when they have known her all of this time and happened to know she did not have it that day. Finally, the only time we feared for Sam on Kea in Hora was when the police made one of their infrequent visits. Their hot rod driving style put every village child in danger. Odette was moved by this series of unprofessional incidents to compose a letter to the editor of one of the major Athenian newspapers.

Much of Italy, the coasts of Spain, as well as the Adriatic Coast of Yugoslavia are guilty of the same kind of mentality that will eventually undercut their whole means of livelihood. Greece is not unique in this disdain for foreigners. But I feel the change more acutely here because of the disruption of the hospitality and mentality that went before the tourist boom.

But in Hora we were simply the xenoi. It is important to note to Greeks who do not live in the city, a xenos can be another Greek: simply not somebody from this very place. By this standard, Athenians are xenoi and so are those on Kithnos, the next island over, or on the mainland around Lavrion. They have not grown up on Kea and are not "like us"!

Those we saw in Hora understood we were not touristes. This became particularly true after mid October when the weather began to turn nasty and the tourist shops had long been boarded up. In fact, there was a mixture of curiosity and respect, perhaps, in the eyes of those we would meet who did not know us well in the village. Some would come out and ask. "What are you doing here?" "How long will you stay?" They respected the fact that I spoke Greek with them, no matter how fragmented and fractured it might be. And their acceptance of us as xenoi came out in different ways: greetings, especially to Sam, as we walked around, and other remarks that acknowledged their awareness of our comings and goings. On one return we stopped to pick up a loaf of bread, and the baker, with whom we had exchanged very few words, said, "Welcome home!"

The truth was, after the middle of October, we were the only non-Greek xenoi living in Hora.

I have no idea how many foreign writers, artists, academics, or what have you may be living in other Greek villages during the winter, but I do know that on some islands there are enough to make up something of a community. Hydra, Aegina, Corfu, Rhodes, Spetsis, Poros, Mykanos, and Crete (which is so large I almost disqualify it as an island!) would all fit this description. In fact, as far back as the mid-1960s, a screenwriting partner, Willard, living with his wife and two children on Rhodes found there were enough xenoi to hire a teacher each year from England to teach the kids in one room of the village schoolhouse in Lindos.

We were, however, the only xenoi family in Hora. This identifies immediately one of the reasons I chose the village: while it is not as isolated as many Greek villages, it is nevertheless not a movie set for rich Athenians and foreigners.

Here we were able to experience the doubleness of being "strangers." We came to feel comfortable, to understand and know much, but not all, about Kean ways. And yet we were not of the island, could never be. Keans, however, had given us a glimpse of that Homeric treatment due foreigners that is fast vanishing as a tradition throughout Greece.

Nothing more clearly captured this spirit for us than our relationship with Argiris and Vasso. One freezing evening we brought them some New Orleans red beans and rice we had cooked up, and they treated us to the beers we had that night. When the phone rang, Vasso spend a good twenty minutes speaking in that loud voice reserved for overseas calls. "It was from Yorghos, the painter in Sweden," she said when she returned. "He wanted to know how we were, that's all." Yorghos was from Athens but taught art in Sweden, bringing students down to Kea from time to time as part of an ongoing program. Thus he is a Greek xenos. "And he wanted to make sure we do plan to visit him in Sweden next year. Imagine that! We have never been out of Greece, but we will go!" she said, laughing her hearty laugh as usual.

"And if you go to Sweden next year, you must make it to New Orleans the year after," Odette had me translate.

"Why not!" she said. "Then we will be the foreigners, the tourists."

"Foreigners, yes," I added, "tourists, no."

Greece Wounds

"Everywhere I go throughout the country," said George Seferis, the Nobel-prize-winning poet, "Greece wounds me."

That expression might surprise some, but not those who come to know more than a summer's vacation about this ancient land.

Others might express it differently. Many I have met would say, "Greece thrills me." Some would definitely say, "Greece pisses me off." And some might combine both: "Greece astonishes me and annoys the hell out of me," one friend said.

My contribution to Seferis' line is not an improvement, but simply a personalizing of my experience. "Everywhere I go, Greece surprises me." I am never bored. There are highs and lows, just like the landscape, and very few level, even-tempered times or places.

For me, "surprise" adds a dash more of hope than Seferis' "wound" suggests. Though I appreciate what his poetry demonstrates clearly: that "wound" means not just the pain of suffering and betrayal, though Greek history is shot through with these themes. But in a broader sense it suggests "being touched deeply," as well.

Two Kinds of People

The Old Man sat at his usual seat in the kafeneon. When he saw me come in and order an ouzo from Kyria Poppy he smiled and gestured me over to his table with his cane.

"Do you know there are two kinds of people in the world?" he asked in his gravel tones.

"Male and female?"

"Of course, my dear man. But beyond that."

"Good and bad?"

"Something more important. I'm speaking of those who live indoors and those who live outdoors."

"Ah!"

"And we Greeks live outdoors."

"That explains a lot."

"Exactly. We spend as little time as possible inside, and we can do that because we have good weather for eight months. You follow me?"

"I follow you."

"Whereas, you take a people like the British, and you can see the way they are because they are inside so much, don't you know?"

"I do. I do."

"We Greeks need to get out, see others, go to the platea, sit in the yard. We seldom invite people over to eat, for instance. We go out to eat, right?"

"Right."

"Whereas an Englishman's home is his castle, so they say. He won't talk to you on the train and saves his best times for what happens when the front door is closed, isn't that so."

"So I've heard. Yes."

"And you, young man, what kind of person are you?"

"An outside person, for sure."

"Where do you live?"

"New Orleans."

The Old Man finished his brandy and smiled.

"Ah, New Orleans. I was there in my youth on a ship. You speak truly. Everybody lives in the streets there. But it is so hot all year."

"Well, only ten months of the year. And it's the humidity, not the heat especially."

"Good point," said the Old Man, treating me to a second ouzo. "That brings up another possibility."

"What's that?" I asked.

"That there are two other kinds of people too."

"Oh, really?"

"Yes. Those who live in dry climates like ours and those who live in humid climates like yours."

"Exactly," I said, working on the octopus hors d'oeuvres.

Stay in Touch

We had no phone on Kea, nor did we want one.

There was always Yannis's store if we wished to call Athens and the OTE telephone office (during working hours till 3 p.m.) if we had to call the States (twice).

Otherwise, staying in touch was by mail, and we became, subsequently, good friends with the young fellows, Babis and Petros, who manned the small post office in Hora. We did not spend hours on correspondence, but bits and pieces of each week did go into the effort. Some was for business reasons, of course: letters of recommendation find their way even to secluded isles, and bills must be paid. But the bulk of our writing went in the form of postcards, notes, letters, Sam's drawings, and articles clipped from here and there, and a few scattered photos to friends in the States and elsewhere.

Babis, age twenty-four and from the small mainland city of Lamia, and Petros, from Hora, also twenty-four, served us well, delighting in Sam's visits too, and informing us whenever we passed on the street, "You have a bunch of letters. Come down!"

Because I came every day, we had a regular conversation, ongoing, on all the subjects that matter–the weather, Greece's European champion basketball team, the prime minister's mistress, life for single young men on Kea (bad!), and "Is Life Better in America or Greece?" (always a stand-off, and we would take turns switching sides). From my first visit to the post office, I was amused by these fellows. That day I found them reading postcards out loud to each other in Greek. How many juicy details have they gleaned in such a manner over the weeks and months they have worked there? I felt safer, however, in English, for while both were enrolled in the Tuesday/Thursday evening English classes offered by the Civilizing Club, neither was proficient enough to crack my scrawled notes.

We have lived abroad before and so have come to treasure the importance of staying in touch with friends. That's part of being abroad, being on an island. We weren't greedy. No long letters needed, but it is good to hear from those we care for and write ourselves.

And we did hear from many we expected to and, as always, those we did not anticipate, a fact that created closer friendships in the process. Most expressed a standardized envy that island life in Greece must be "ideal." These were friends who have seen only the travel posters and have not dealt with the balancing frustrations that make up life anywhere. Others, such as Mike, my friend in New York who has been there (Greece) twice before and majored in ancient Greek in college before becoming a New York lawyer who keeps Plato in his bathroom, wrote with greater clarity of our reality: "Your life there sounds wonderful, but my experience leads me to say it must really be like camping out. While you describe the joys of swimming and hiking, you are strangely silent on the subject of plumbing." Of course, he was right. But we would wait till we saw him at Christmas in person to tell him that the plumbing was so "dicey" that all papers had to be placed in the covered waste can by the toilet. That alone would have kept him from visiting us, for sure!

It's good to hear gossip from home and work, both to look forward to what you missed, and to feel relief at what you do not have to face. Thus we appreciated people such as Odette's brother, Marc, who would clip out interesting and silly pieces from New Orleans' inimitable attempt at a paper, *The Times Picayune*, and send them along.

But there was one note of distress that cropped up time and again in correspondence. It was that strained voice of hurried lives being lived on the run without time for pleasure, peace, pause. "Would like to say more but have to run." "I'm working too hard, but hope to slow down next year." "Between teaching, committee meetings, tenure and promotion procedures and my academic writing projects, no time to even watch the news on TV." And so on. The level of quiet and not so quiet desperation in these letters seemed even more amplified in the rural peace of Kea. Of course, we too would soon be returning to "the real world," but we spent a fair amount of time discussing how "the spirit of Kea" would carry over into daily life "back home." It would be a challenge.

The most distressing letters and cards of all, however, were those that never came. I am speaking of those we consider "good friends," almost all of whom have known us long enough to have written to us the last time we were abroad for six months and/or people we have done much for, professionally and otherwise. Their silence was puzzling and troubling.

I've learned over the years that some people just don't write. Many Greek friends are in this category. But while this may annoy us, at least we can deal with it if we know they are this way. Yet people who have written in the past, who know the importance of staying in touch, to whom we have ourselves written time and again, often with specific questions we needed answered, are something else. "Eliminate negative thoughts," commands one Seeker of Inner Peace. And she is right. But I do not think it is negative to realize a lesson that Greece has taught me over the past twenty-one years: There are friends and there are colleagues at work, and there are acquaintances, each is distinct and different, and one can move from one kind to another over time.

Friendship is a central issue for the ancients, time and again. Euripides is very specific:

"Nothing's more precious than a loyal friend.
Not wealth, not kingship. A whole city to command is worthless,
Weighed against one honorable friend."

                                    –Orestes

I have found in America the illusion that one has or should have "many" friends. My Greek roommate in college, Dimitri, laughed every time he heard someone speak of having lots of "close" friends. "A friend is someone you would do anything for at any time," he said. "How many of your `friends' will do that?" Not many. "Everyone else is an acquaintance," he said, "someone you know, have a good time with, see at work, are pleasant to, but not that you can depend on, not who will come through for you and understand you and support you." Dimitri said he was lucky: he had two friends!

My standards are not as severe. I'd like to think I have at least double Dimitri's number of friends. But living on Kea did make us see more clearly who bothered to stay in touch and who didn't. Dimitri is right to a point. What passes for friendship is often convenience. We once noticed that a couple we enjoyed and had over for numerous evenings never called or returned the favor. We weren't asking much: just a simple two-way form of communication within the same city. For the hell of it, we decided not to call them until they called us, to see if, in fact, our desire to be friends was simply an illusion or not. It was. Four years have passed, and the phone hasn't rung nor have we seen them. Similarly, the silence from some we considered friends who used to write and who have, as far as we know, no excuse for not writing and for whom we have gone more than the extra mile to help is pause for reflection before returning home. Out of sight, out of mind is not a firm foundation for any relationship, as Dimitri made clear.

Kea and the Blue Ridge Mountains of Virginia

The more we stayed on Kea, the more I realized certain affinities between the island and my home territory of the Blue Ridge Mountains of Virginia.

Though I have not lived for long continuous stretches in Virginia, I was born there and I spent many childhood summers and numerous other occasions at my grandparents' home in the Shenandoah Valley. The "Valley," as it is known, has always had a calming effect on me, not just because of the relaxed freedom offered one by grandparents but also because the Valley has managed to remain one of the few truly beautiful, nonindustrialized areas of the United States.

Like Kea, the Valley is still predominantly agricultural and rural. But also like Kea, the nature of rural life has changed drastically in the past twenty years or so. If anything, a Kean farmer and a Valley farmer would have much more in common to talk about these days than ever before. Beyond talk of mountain life and crop and livestock raising, the Toyota driving Kean and the van owning Virginian would also be chatting about selling land to rich city folk (the Washington, D.C., crowd for the Virginians or even rich Germans and Japanese), video recorders and rented tapes, government price supports, and the changing futures of their children.

But apart from similarities of size and geography, another point of comparison struck me on Kea. Both Greece and my area of Virginia are examples of a classless society. I suppose I had known this intellectually before, but the reality of this fact only sunk in living on Kea on a day-to-day basis.

Four hundred years under the Turks reduced all Greeks to more or less one social class. Gone were the divisions so apparent in the Byzantine Empire between rich and poor. But even during the Byzantine period, the aristocracy was not always hereditary, as I have already suggested. There was then, as there is today in Greece, a chance for the enterprising individual to advance and rise. The classlessness of modern Greece is more difficult to sense in Athens where the nouveau riche have become established enough with their mansions in Kiffisia and fancy apartments in Kolonaki. But the Socialist government of Papandreou has, at least, since it came to power in 1980, seen to it that many of those who might have been labeled as a Greek "aristocracy" from old families and moneyed parents have been replaced by talented professionals in various fields with simple backgrounds.

Similarly, while the United States began in part as a rebellion against the kinds of stratified social structure so apparent in England, the country has developed clear class lines determined by wealth and power. But in the Shenandoah Valley, and particularly in towns such as the one in which my grandparents lived, a very real sense of classlessness still exists. There is no huge distance between the fanciest house in their town and the poorer ones (though there is now a distressing subclass of "trailer people" springing up along mountain roads).

And the same is true of Kea. Nobody in Hora is very wealthy, and extreme poverty is also absent. The only fancy home in the town, completed while we were there, was so ostentatious, so gaudy, that it served as a butt of jokes rather than a point of envy. No one took such a tawdry display of money seriously.

Marxist regimes always speak of a classless society, but none has created one. Each socialist country I have visited has created an aristocracy of power for the ruling elite. But the truly classless state of Kea also made me aware of the depressing gap between the haves and have-nots in my more immediate backyard: New Orleans. Time apart on Kea helped me realize even more clearly how far the old rich white families of the city exist from the poor blacks, whites and others, not just in life style and financial terms, but in terms of attitude as well. On Kea we were free, for a time, from the often subtle reality of social snobbery that a highly class-oriented society like that of New Orleans breeds, a snobbery that, ironically, even extends within black culture itself as old creole families look down their noses at poorer and blacker families who have not had the advantages they have had.

On Kea I was grateful to experience a social structure in which the mayor was a cab driver, the banker a general store manager, and where even the bakers were also farmers. As more money pours into the island, however, even this delicate balance, maintained for so many centuries, will change. Or will it? I hope to return again and again for years to see if such a sense of equality can survive.

Winter Blues

One freezing November afternoon we hit bottom.

Sam began throwing his toys around the house.

"I hate my toys. I hate the house. I hate Mommy and I hate Daddy. I hate Sam. I hate Kea. I hate New Orleans. I hate everybody. I hate everything."

Cold rains and gale force winds had kept us inside for three days without heat. The temperature hovered in the low 40s, but the lashing winds made it even colder, and dampness meant the sheets were sticky, towels never dried, mold began to grow on the cane-bottomed chairs.

We were depressed.

And frozen.

This was no way for us to live, but especially, no way for a child to be. We all caught colds.

What had gone wrong?

Lou had done his damnedest. By mid-October, before the weather turned nasty, he had brought a fine old cast-iron, brand new Franklin stove from Athens. But it had been delivered to a worker's home above the village, and the worker had been busy and then sick and then busy again. So the stove sat up above us a few hundred meters for over three weeks while the rains fell, the temperatures collapsed, and the winds rose.

Yet just before we had headed for Athens to hear Jon and Eddie play the blues, the worker had knocked on our door and carried in the stove off of his donkey. We had a stove-heater!

But we did not have the connecting metal pipes leading from the stove up and out of the upstairs room to the outside. A certain Yorghos was the man for the job, and he too was "busy" and then sick and then busy again. Lou called him nightly, and I called during the day. No luck. "My child is freezing. Please help!" I'd say, and he'd promise to come, and we'd stay home, but Yorghos never showed.

One day that we considered just giving up, packing up and heading back to Athens for good, the boat didn't come: the winds were over forty miles per hour, and like it or not we were stuck.

For the first time ever for any of us, our top priority was simple survival. I don't mean in any dramatic sense of life against death. But our overriding concern was to keep ourselves warm enough to make it through this unusually cold and windy spell. Odette and Sam coped by spending even more time under covers, while I did my work on the typewriter wearing gloves. We each wore shirt upon shirt with sweaters on top and double socks. Still, we were miserable.

When it was just cold, with no rain, I insisted that we combat cabin fever with short walks out of the village. One day, it was past the Lion of Kea to another small church we had never taken in before. And another day I took Sam up above the town to the top of the ridge where the skeletons of some fifteen or more windmills stand. But the wind was so strong that Sam literally could not walk forward against it, and a peasant came out of his way with his donkey to instruct me in my duty to get my child home before he died of the cold.

I felt terrible. Before we had returned to Kea after the blues concert, Dimitri and Katerina, with whom we stayed in Athens, urged and then insisted that we should not return. "You will be miserable there. Why go?" said Dimitri, who had been particularly miserable when he came several weeks before, and it had been only mildly cold and uncomfortable. I had expected a sudden pleasant change in the weather. It had not come, and I felt guilty. After all, I was the one who had insisted on dragging us into the cold.

Partially, I had been counting on Yorghos finally coming through. He had "promised" to finish putting in the pipes while we were in Athens for three days, and I had left the key to the house with Yannis for that exact purpose.

But to our dismay, nothing had been done.

One night in particular was the worst. We had, as usual, drawn out supper at Argiris' as long as we could, trying both to enjoy being out of the house and also basking in the relatively warmer environment of the taverna (though Argiris left an upper window open, even on the coldest days). But once back through the rain and in bed, down below in our room, Sam nuzzled in between us rather than in his own bed, we lay there in the dark hearing a wind howl, bash and blow as we had never heard one before. All night long the noise was deafening. And as the wind gathered speed and whipped down the street outside our bedroom door, we had the feeling the doors and windows would all cave in to the force that battered them mercilessly.

If we had heat, even that night could have been transformed into an "adventure," but such was not the case. We were trembling, frozen, frightened.

Part of the reason to spend so much time on an island was to take in the change in seasons. But I had not bargained for so much, and certainly not for a house without any heating. We are not spoiled. Central heating is not a necessity. Our New Orleans home features old-fashioned open space gas heaters in only two of our five rooms, so we are used to making do with variable temperatures. Yet during that three-day stretch, I had my serious doubts about winter island life with a child.

The next day was cold, but the winds had moved on and the sky was luminously clear. Our spirits improved.

And that evening at Argiris', a solution to our situation appeared. I had, the previous night, marched into the kafeneon when told that Yorghos was there. Since my calls and Lou's had brought no results, and pleas for our child's health had not won him over to doing a job he should have done several weeks before (he had truly been sick, but still, he had been well enough to work on other projects since then), I needed to take direct action. The kafeneon is, of course, the center of male camaraderie, thus I was counting on shaming Yorghos into coming.

Shame is a stronger power than guilt in Greece because it depends on defending personal honor rather than a generalized religious standard. So I wandered into the crowded coffee shop–in a scene not unlike a bad Western– and went up to Yorghos, who was playing cards at one of the two large card tables. The good-humored fellow who had brought down the somba (heater) on his donkey smiled and said, "You must be freezing, right? Especially your boy!" I nodded, and those present, who recognized me and had clearly heard the story before, pointed to Yorghos and groaned a groan that acknowledged Yorghos's culpability. Yorghos looked sheepish and a bit drunk. I said nothing. I simply patted his shoulder and said, "So tomorrow, okay Yorghos?" "Tomorrow. Of course," he replied, and I left, as the group continued to haze Yorghos in good-natured fun.

Surely such a public shaming in that center of male culture would do the trick! Surely he could not now back down. Wrong.

Yorghos never showed.

But the night I am speaking of at Argiris', the young fellow with a beard, also a Yorghos, who came in after English lessons to study, chat, and watch TV, was there. He listened as I unwound and, yes, embellished our tale of woe.

A quiet fellow of twenty-six, single, with sparkling eyes and a shy smile, he simply added, "I'll do it." And that was that. He was to follow us home, take the measurements and bring the pipes the following day. He was a builder, not an installer of heating pipes, but builders on Kea know a bit about everything.

On the way up to the house, however, we ran into Yorghos number 1. He could not look us straight in the eye and made a thousand apologies for Sam freezing. Young Yorghos cut through all of this. "Look. I'll do it." That did it: a colleague's intervention. He would never live that one down. "No. No. I can put in the pipe inside, but I'm still too sick to work outside." "Okay," said the young Yorghos, "you put in the inside pipe tomorrow and by six when I'm off work, I'll come around and finish off the outside."

And that's almost exactly what happened.

Once the outside fixtures were in place, Yorghos number 1 left. We poured a glass of wine for Yorghos number 2, and he helped us build our first fire. Heat radiated throughout our small room, warming and drying the place almost instantly. We toasted the occasion and Yorghos's good will and felt like survivors. Sam's mood, already improved by the sunshine, became even better as he poured his attention and curiosity into learning all about a wood-burning stove.

Wood?

Yes. But that had been another story. Three weeks before, a donkey had arrived with a load of firewood for us, everything from sticks to sawed logs. And we had stored it all neatly in the downstairs hallway in anticipation of our small Franklin stove.

Now, near the middle of November, a few weeks before our departure, we were warm once again.

Flora

"Hello. I see you with your camera.... My door? Ah, the lace embroidery in the window of the door! I am proud of it. At eighty I can still embroider well.... And me too? Well, why not. I've seen you go by many times from my little room with your child. A girl or a boy. A boy! May he live to be a hundred!...Come on in, I want to show you something. That's it, come in. Yes, I live in this one room, my bed there, my souvenirs on the wall and family pictures and icon, of course, wardrobe.... I don't need much! Oh, I have a large house nearby, but at my age what would I do with it? So I have given it to my daughter. She lives there, and I visit all the time.... Yes, right, that's my radio, not new, but it works fine. I like that classical station from Athens, listen to it while I knit or embroider, don't really read much anymore. But I wanted you to see this, yes, the photo of me standing here in my room! A foreigner took it, look, it was this summer, here's the envelope, can you read foreign languages? You must be able to. Where did you say you were from? Ah, America!.... What did you say? Austria? Oh, now I remember, she did say she was from up there somewheres, but nice of her to send me one, right? Do you want to take a picture in here? No flash, I see, maybe another time. Stop on by, I never go anywhere, and you can see me day and night from the street through my one window. Name? Flora. Yes, it is unusual in Greece. Like flowers, isn't it!"

Socrates, Euripides and Tadeusz Borowski

Socrates died drinking hemlock assigned him by the state. He had defended himself in court as best he could but lost his case. Believing both that one should obey the laws of one's state or leave, and also believing that no harm could come to a man because the soul is immortal, he calmly spoke with his friends and family, bid them farewell and drank his death.

Such was the life of a philosopher who believed in rationality and eternal forms beyond the flux of life.

Euripides believed quite the opposite and died, reportedly, murdered by bacchants, women devoted to Dionysios, who accused him of giving away too many secrets of their frenzied and mystical ceremonies in his last play, *The Bacchae.* Euripides was the poet of passion and passion's excesses. As an old man living in Macedonia, his thoughts turned not to rationality or immortality, but to the dark, irrational powers within man. "'Tis a majestic thing, the darkness," he wrote in his powerful evocation of Dionysios, his cult, his ecstasy and destructive forces. And Euripides was destroyed by those same forces.

Such was the life of a playwright aware of the dark face of passion.

Tadeusz Borowski was a Polish writer who lived through the horror of the concentration camps in World War II and wrote about them in chillingly perceptive stories I read on Kea. He committed suicide on July 1st, 1951, at the age of twenty-nine, ironically by turning on the gas in his Warsaw apartment. Auschwitz taught him that there have always been two types of people: executioners and victims. In his most desperate moment he wrote, "The living are always right, the dead are always wrong."

Neither Socrates nor Euripides chose death, yet each died according to his beliefs. Their opposite views span the complete diversity of Greek culture, well suggested by Nietzsche in his discussion of the forces of Apollo (order, mind, light) and Dionysios (disorder, passion, darkness).

The unfolding of the twentieth century has given us a perspective neither ancient could have imagined: two World Wars and numerous others, atomic mass murder, world famine, and, as in the case of the concentration camps, willful and systematic destruction of whole peoples by the millions.

Borowski lived through this all and chose to die. By his own words, that makes him wrong now. Yet his words live on in his writings. This is the power of literature, of philosophy, of drama. We, the living, have to shoulder the weight of it all and continue. We search for our peace: the dead have found theirs.

"Plato lied," wrote Borowski in one story.

If so, the dark face of Dionysios looms ever more clearly over us all.

Winter, Rainbows and Frozen Fish

Greeks started wishing each other "happy winter" after the Feast of the Panayea on August 15th.

But for me it officially arrived the morning of October 13th when I awoke to a thunderstorm. Rain pounded our roof for the first time, lightening filled the sky and the wind lashed away at our doors and windows.

For the first time, we felt wintery. I got out my new Greek sweater, put on the coffee, and thought of lentil soup.

By noon, however, there was a rainbow over the sea, and a stunning one at that. I rushed in to get Odette and Sam to witness the brightest one I had ever seen. Rising out of dark clouds, it stretched clear from the island of Eubea to our right to the far end of Makronisos far to the left. Sam was amazed. It was his first.

Shortly after, all clouds disappeared and sweaters were discarded.

A perfect day!

It was as if Nature had found the gold mean that the ancients had so long sought but seldom achieved.

On the way to supper that evening to celebrate such a coming in of winter, we stopped in at Yannis's to buy a few things. Argiris came in asking for frozen fish.

"Who died?" was once again Yannis' question.

"Good old Frankos," Argiris replied.

Everyone expressed surprise but not deep grief. Frankos was in his 70s and went quickly: his heart.

While we headed for Argiris' to eat stuffed eggplant, fried small fish and lamb in lemon sauce, Argiris gathered up enough frozen fish for the next evening's makarea for Good Old Frankos.

"150 people," Argiris said. "35 kilos should do it."

Students Who Become Friends

When I came to Greece fresh from college in 1966, I had no desire whatsoever to become a teacher. I took a one-year position as a "teaching fellow" at Athens College, an American organized and managed private school for males (it has since gone coed), to gain time to think over what I wanted to do. And I came for two other reasons: I had had a Greek roommate at Hamilton College, Dimitri, and he kindled my interest in seeing Greece, an interest that was not so much based on a love of Classical literature and language as it was for contemporary and modern influences. I enjoyed the novels of Nikos Kazantzakis and Lawrence Durrell's writings about Greece, as well as Henry Miller's *Colossus of Maroussi*, his vivid recreation of Greece on the verge of World War II as he traveled with Lawrence Durrell and met many of the literary giants of modern Greece. My final reason for coming had to do with Viet Nam. I was against the war there and yet wanted, as a first course of action, to try and do something "constructive" instead of shooting people for a cause I could not accept. My draft board judged teaching in Greece as legitimate, and I packed my bags.

But teaching was simply a means to an end, not the goal itself.

As it turned out, I discovered I loved the classroom and the contact with students in and out of the academic environment. That pleasure led me to return to graduate school for an M.A. degree and then on for the Ph.D., returning in 1973 to teach again in Greece, and, after 1976, in the United States at the university level.

Certainly a valued dimension of being a teacher for me has been to have classroom contacts turn into friendships after the final exams for European Cinema or Contemporary Fiction or World Classics or whatever other course I've taught are long forgotten. And my return to Greece and stay on Kea brought one very special pleasure: renewed friendships with former Greek students with whom I have stayed in touch for over twelve years.

Coming "home" after twenty-one years, therefore, concerned not just Greece but also my chosen profession. And these ex-student friendships definitely made me feel good about my years in the classroom, the library, and at the typewriter. Much about teaching these days is discouraging. No need to troupe out the long list of complaints from byzantine administrative structures and poor pay to "dirty politics" of an intensity unknown even in jaded Washington, D.C., and unreasonable demands on one's time. No matter these issues for now. What did matter for me on Kea was that seeing Penny, Klety, Spyros, Ariane, Nikos, Dimitri, Evris, and others again reminded me about that special spark that begins in a classroom where real intellectual curiosity and dialogue is begun and which can grow with years.

I do not take credit for my former students' success (or failures). But I do take pride in seeing talents and passions I had recognized years ago take hold, take shape, bloom. For that reason I'm always surprised at colleagues who drift through year after year of teaching without ever knowing what has happened to any of their past students. Such self absorption with subject matter alone seems to me to run contrary to the essence of education, at least as it has come down to us from the Greeks. Remember that Plato was Socrates' student and that Aristotle studied under Plato. "Teacher-student" is not a clear enough label for the levels for communication and sharing and caring that developed, in this case, between and among these three remarkable men.

I value each for what they are, so a description of what they have done or are doing is only part of what they have become.

Penny I have mentioned in relation to her mother, Poppy, and our stay on Poros. She has completed an M.A. in American literature from one British university and, besides being a mother and wife, is busy completing a Ph.D. in American literature at Cambridge. With Penny and Costas–her husband–we not only had "academic" matters to discuss, but through many evenings and numerous morning coffee gatherings we had the fun of letting Kallissa, their daughter, and Sam get together to play.

Spyros has completed his Ph.D. in English literature from a British university with a thesis on the poetry of Yeats, some of which he has translated into Greek. He and his longtime friend, Xanthi, married some six years ago and also have a bright-eyed four-and-a-half year-old daughter. Spyros is presently teaching at a newly formed university on Corfu, and he is translating as well.

Klety was divorced with two young sons when I knew her some fourteen years ago. Her interest in South American literature began, she claims, in one of my classes on contemporary fiction, and continued as she studied in England, married Eduardo, a Columbian who has since become a diplomat, presently (and conveniently) assigned to Greece. Klety's love of literature has found full expression in translation. She has translated thirteen Spanish and Latin American novels into Greek, making her the major Spanish language translator of literature in Greece. Her specialty has been Gabriel Garcia Marquez whom she began translating as an assignment in my class. While we were in Greece, Klety had begun to teach at the same American-run university at which I had taught. Pleasant to see the cycle turn full circle.

Ariane has been in close contact since leaving the university I taught at in

Greece. With an American mother and a Greek father, it was appropriate that she completed her B.A. at a major American university. After that she returned to teach in an unusual program for American students with two "campuses." One is the island of Kalymnos, the only remaining "sponge diving" island in Greece, and the other was in Metsovo, an intriguing mountain village in Epirus, not far from the Albanian border. Deciding against an academic career, however, she turned to "media," completed the Greek film school while working with Dimitri, our television director friend whom we met through her. She is presently on scholarship in her second year at the very tough and respected New York University Film School. Her career in film and television seems certain.

Film is also the profession of several other students I had who took my "Film and Literature" course, the first such course in Greece back between 1974 and 1976. What memories I have of lugging heavy 35mm prints of movies around Athens from the distributors to the college in my beat-up VW to project in a huge auditorium on an ancient arc-light projector.

Other students I wonder about have "disappeared." And ones I don't remember come up from time to time (one has become a well-known actor). But so it goes in teaching as in life.

And those times I thought about teaching while on Kea, I wondered about something else. Why has it been that more lasting friendships have developed with my former Greek students than with American students? I'm the same professor teaching the same way with what I hope is my same energy level and concern in each place, but the American connections have, in general, not lasted as long or with as much pleasant intensity.

Easy answers might have to do with America as a more mobile society where people move and drop and make friends constantly. But harder answers would have to deal with different perceptions of learning and personal relationships that exist in different cultures.

I am not the only one in the profession to notice this. I have often discussed with colleagues at several institutions in the United States what I call the "zombie effect." I refer to spending a semester with students and getting to "know" them to the degree that is possible in a classroom (and one learns a lot more about each other than might seem possible at first). They attend class, they join in discussions (I never just "lecture"), they are forced to express themselves as clearly as they can in writing about things that should matter to them. And then when the course is over and you pass them on campus, there is the glazed-over look of a zombie, the look of someone who's not there, a person who, for whatever reason, is showing no recognition of you (me), no suggestion of memory that a semester together in dialogue and common discussion has taken place.

I don't recall this "zombie effect" ever happening to me in Greece or Yugoslavia or the other countries where I have taught and spoken.

There are no easy answers as to what this means. And surely I have had enough fine students in the United States each year to feel stimulated and concerned and willing to give whatever help I can. But I do remain with many questions. And one of them is this: what does it mean for a country to "educate" people who are bright enough to pass exams and get degrees but who have somehow missed the spirit and the essence of what learning and existing in a social group offers?

Anarchy and Individualism

My first year in Greece I traveled by local bus towards Delphi with four other teaching friends. We got to Thebes with no trouble, but when it appeared we would have to wait for hours to go the final stretch through the mountains to Delphi, we all chipped in and found an obliging taxi driver.

What we didn't fully realize was that it was against the law to have more than four passengers in a cab. The driver, a stocky, mustached fellow in his late forties, seemed not to care a fig about this problem, so we soon found ourselves moving swiftly along a winding road approaching Mount Parnassos, the famed home of the Muses.

Out of nowhere a motorcycle cop appeared and flagged down our taxi. Wearing sunglasses even though it was a cloudy day, the patrolman wrote out a ticket to the driver, informed him he had been breaking the law and handed him the ticket. The driver looked at the policeman, tore the ticket into pieces, dropped them outside the window, and as he pulled away leaving the officer standing there, he shouted, "Give the ticket to your mother instead!" Our last view of the man was of him standing there, stunned and seemingly helpless.

That early experience was an important one, for it was a preview of many similar variations of confrontations and modes of behavior I have come to understand as part and parcel of Greek character.

The cabbie's action was a radiant example of a mixture of anarchy and individualism that has always been seen in Greece. Surely, in most places, the driver would have taken and paid the ticket, perhaps with some strong verbal exchanges being made, but still, ultimately, following procedures. Not so for our Greek taxi driver. Yes, he seemed say, he had technically broken the law. But what the hell. What real harm had been done? And who was this officer to be so picky and so smug in chasing him down in the middle of an isolated highway! It was an affront to him as a person, as an individual, as a citizen! Yes, he might now get in three times as much trouble for thumbing his nose at the law and the authorities. But, for the taxi driver, it was clearly worth the risk.

We never learned what finally happened, and as the driver let us off at Delphi, the Center of the Universe for the ancients, he seemed not a bit worried about the consequences.

Anarchy and individualism. The Greeks have given us the concept of the city-state–the polis–and democracy–the rule of public affairs by the people of the city. And they have provided us with a sense of the worth of the individual. But how complex a reality individualism is in Greece only became clearer to me through the years of living there.

The Greeks like to tell a nationality joke which goes something like this. One Englishman, fool, two Englishmen, a club, and three Englishmen, a colony. One German, a scientist, two Germans, a beer garden, and three Germans, a war. And so on till we come to the Greeks. One Greek, one prime minister, two Greeks, two prime ministers, and three Greeks, three prime ministers.

No man is an island, but every Greek is a complete universe unto him/herself.

The first year I taught in Greece, I had a ninth-grade class in English. I remember that time and time again I would ask a question and hands would shoot up. Perhaps Socrates would answer it, but three hands were still up. When I called on Pericles, he gave the same answer, as did Nikos, and Dimitri after him. When I informed each that that answer had just been given, they seemed surprised; they had not been listening. What mattered was that they each had the answer and wanted to be recognized in such a role. While such behavior was generally amusing to me in the classroom, multiplied at a national level the possibilities for conflict and confusion become apparent.

Certainly a sense of individuality has been important throughout Greek history. From Odysseus to Onassis, and from Helen to Melina Mercouri, Greeks have stood out clearly as individual personalities, characters, talents. And a sense of abandon often bordering on anarchy has often been useful as well. Onassis did not become a shipping tycoon by investing in government savings bonds, and the Greeks did not beat Xerxes' powerful army in hand-to-hand combat on the battlefield. Cleverness, and an ability to take risks, risks that often seemed foolish to others, often paid off.

Personally I have learned much about the "healthy" need for some degree of "anarchy" in our daily lives so that we do not become programmed zombies in a post-industrial state. Melina Mercouri's popular role as the large-hearted, hot-blooded prostitute in *Never on Sunday* is but one feisty example of such a spirit of individualism which refuses to be crushed under social customs and unreasonable rules.

At its best, therefore, such anarchy is a live affirming vote for the worth of the single person. A beautiful moment in modern Greek cinema reiterates this as a Greek actor in Theodore Angelopoulos' *The Traveling Players* (1975) is about to be shot by a German firing squad during the Occupation. We see an establishing long shot of the soldiers and the actor in an isolated field. Suddenly the camera goes into a close-up of the actor who faces the camera (thus putting us in the position of the firing squad) and tells us his name and where he is from and what he does, the typical information that one always gives to strangers in Greece. And then he simply says, "And you...who are you?" There is a quick cut to another long shot, the soldiers fire, and the actor slumps to the earth. What Angelopoulos so simply and powerfully does is to make us experience the individuality of this man and the naturalness of his curiosity about "us," other human individuals (even the firing squad), before he becomes a non-person, a corpse.

The negative side of such a strong concept of self is equally complex but real. On Kea we ran into various examples ranging from the humorous to the absolutely infuriating. It was funny to hear of one lady who had asked a plumber to fix the gutters on her roof only to have the man say he would be back when he got the right parts. Two years later he showed up as if nothing had happened and was offended when the lady became angry. But it was not so funny to us that we could not get the plumber to install heating pipes for us even after explaining to him time and time again that we and our child were sick with colds because we had no heat. The point was, he would get to it when he wanted.

But in an ironic sense, Odette and I came to realize that in this matter of anarchy and selfhood, New Orleans and Greece are not so far apart. One friend of ours who moved to New Orleans several years ago from Salt Lake City, Utah says it best. "When I first came to New Orleans, I was upset almost every day. Nothing seemed to go right. People never showed up on time, didn't return calls, made promises they didn't keep, kept hours that made no sense to me, and so on. The result was that my marriage fell apart and I quit my '9 to 5' job. But then I woke up one morning and suddenly realized. Hey, New Orleans is not the United States. This is its own country with its own attitudes and ways of doing things. From that moment on, New Orleans was the only place I could live happily."

Much of the same is true for and of Greece. When the Anglo-Saxon spirit runs into the Mediterranean Greek spirit, clashes are bound to spring up if some understanding and acceptance of a different perspective and attitude toward self and society is not taken into account. After all, history has shown Greeks seldom agree with Greeks. Thus, it is natural to expect extra-national conflicts if something of the delicate balance between order and chaos, tradition and anarchy, self and individualism are not appreciated.

Pasteli

"What should we take away with us as a souvenir of Kea?" one foreign friend asked.

"Pasteli," I said.

Pasteli is island honey mixed with sesame seeds. You can buy pasteli other places, but it is always brick hard and usually mixed with generous portions of sugar. On Kea the pasteli is pure honey and seeds. Thus it is always pliable, chewable.

This is not the kind of sweet that usually interests me, but one bite and I was hooked. I was pleased to see how devoted friends also became to whom we gave pasteli when visiting Athens.

And to buy it, I had to tell the old lady in the sweets shop how many boxes I wanted and then return later after she had wrapped the strips of pasteli and stuffed them in small boxes and wrapped the boxes. Clearly, Kea was making no effort to mass produce its front running delicacy.

Like the island itself, Kean pasteli was only for those who knew about it and took the time to go after it.

"I Did It by Myself"

On Kea, Sam grew in independence. "I did it by myself," was a phrase he loved to exercise.

The time it had the most meaning for us, however, was when he did his first shopping for us at Yannis's, alone.

By late October, Sam knew the village so well, and he in turn was so well known by the village, that we decided to send him alone the block and a half of twisted, turning streets to Yannis's to fetch a jar of fresh island honey. We gave him some money, an empty jar and a note in Greek that read, "Yannis, honey, please."

Sam set off with great pride, looking back once to say, "Stay there. Don't follow me!"

We went inside and made a pot of coffee.

A few minutes later, the door opened, Sam entered with a huge smile on his face, handed us the honey and change, and announced, "I got the honey by myself!"

Other trips to Yannis's followed before we left. But that chilly October morning when Sam first undertook a solo shopping spree was a happy day.

"We could never let him do this at his age back home," Odette lamented. "He'd get run over or kidnapped or worse."

"Or at least we would worry that he would," I added.

Winter Hikes

When swimming became impossible, hiking season began.

Hiking with Sam, of course, meant we had to map out our excursions carefully, planning either to walk one way and taxi home, or to choose a round trip which we felt we could handle should we have to carry him most of the way.

Still, within these stipulations, we managed many pleasant wanderings.

A simple route was just outside the village below the cemetery to the blackberry bushes. An hour passed like a flash as Sam focused all of his attention on pointing out to us the difficulty in reaching berries.

Other times we would look around and hike to a countryside chapel we had not yet visited before, light a candle, and return.

And when we lacked imagination, the walk down to the harbor was always pleasant enough, especially since it includes a mile of stone pathway, the original road, away from the main highway.

But the hikes we enjoyed most were on the splendid network of stone paths lined with stone walls which are etched throughout the island and punctuated with springs along the way and an ever-changing view of the sea and the island itself.

How truly agricultural an island Kea is also becomes apparent hiking these stone trails. On one hike along the paved highway towards Pices one day, two cars passed us in an hour. But an hour's walking on stone paths would always bring us in contact with close to a dozen folk, either riding donkeys, walking along, working in the fields, tending animals.

But one of my favorite hikes was shared with an Irish friend, Mike, and his German friend, Martje. We took turns carrying Sam on a longish trek inland to an abandoned monastery on top of a hill. The day was cold and blustery. The view, with dark clouds over the grey sea, was dramatic. We reached the ruins to find, happily, that the main church was open. Inside, the dim winter light shone on the ikons at the front of the church. We lit candles, and then Martje began to sing some Handel. The acoustics were perfect. Her voice reverberated throughout the interior, echoing memories of what it must have been like when monks chanted the beautiful Byzantine hymns.

Then Sam began to sing, at first faintly, then with bravado, working his own variation on Snow White's classic: "Some day my QUEEN will come, some day my QUEEN will come!"

Handel and Disney met, blended, and filled the winter air of an isolated church dedicated to the Virgin high on a hill on Kea that day.

Argiris and Vasso Revisited

We spent so much time at Argiris' taverna that we practically became family. Especially enjoyable were weekday nights when we were often just about the only souls around and often the only customers.

Take one cold night in late October.

Vasso had a plastic container full of raisin jam for Sam, a returned gift for Sam's previous night's gift to Vasso: a bunch of his favorite sweet, "peanut butter balls" (rolled peanut butter, powdered milk, honey, and shredded coconut on the outside).

Argiris was watching a documentary on the Greek defeat of the Italian forces in 1940 in Northern Greece. This led me to ask about Kea during World War II. Argiris was just a baby, but he spoke of the Italians controlling the island. His home is at the furthermost tip of the island, near the lighthouse that looks out over the ten or so miles to Kithnos. The Italians set up a watch point there since so many ships sail between the two islands on their way elsewhere. Were the Italians as brutal as the Germans? "No massacres or anything like that," he said, "and even though we had to give them our cattle and sheep, we could always find garlic and onions and mountain greens to eat. All in all, we had it better than the poor folk in Athens and elsewhere."

Setting up the table had its rituals. Kyria Vasso or Argiris brought out the bread and silverware basket with their smallest fork saved for Sam. And I would go into the kitchen and bring out the glasses, including water for Sam, and open a bottle of retsina for us.

With only a month left on the island, I found myself asking how difficult it would be to get to the lighthouse and his home where his deaf brother lives. He started to explain and then he said, "I tell you what. One of these Sundays, let's go all together and spend the night. You can look around and we'll come back." I was pleased. And I began to look forward to this last long island journey.

Meanwhile, Sam, who seldom sat still in Argiris', had found a broom outside and had begun sweeping up leaves and candy wrappers. From time to time he would return for chicken or feta cheese or bread dipped in olive oil.

At one point a very formal and snooty Athenian couple in their fifties opened the door and asked Argiris if he had fish. "Yes." "Big fish?" "No," he said with indifference and with no effort to sell them any other pitch about the place. They left and went next door to a mediocre meal in a larger room with less atmosphere.

Then a young fellow, strong as fifty mules, a builder and mule driver, came in carrying what I recognized as English lesson books for the course being run by the village school teacher as a service of the Civilizing Club.

He stationed himself at the table between Argiris, who was now reading the paper, and Vasso, who was watching a silly melodrama on TV. He ordered only a Pepsi and set about earnestly doing his English homework.

The phone rang and Vasso announced it was for me. That had never happened before. Penny and Costa in Athens were calling that they could not come for the weekend, a call that was, I figured out, only possible because they called Lou and Judy first to get Argiris' number.

Argiris went next door to his grocery to get a few things and came back, past the fifty-pound sack of garlic propped near the door, and stopped at our table. "Sam has done a great job of sweeping out there. Tomorrow I will speak with the mayor and see if we can get him not only the official job of street sweeper, but get him Social Security and Blue Cross as well!"

And before we left, Vasso brought over a small plate of keftedes (meatballs) and chips, another gift for Sam. "For my friend Sam," she said with the smile that seldom seemed to leave her face.

Departures

Leaving Kea is never easy.

Even when we truly had things we wanted to do–people we looked forward to seeing on the mainland–still, at the last minute, hesitancy would set in. Couldn't we wait another week, a few more days? And sometimes we did. Odette, in fact, went for three weeks without leaving.

Yes, an island is limited. There is only the territory clearly surrounded on all sides by sea, and the inhabitants do not shuffle about as often or as nervously as do mainlanders. Still something hurt every time I saw the harbor fade away. There is the illusion of safety and completeness on an island, and to leave it is to go into a much larger world that seems to have no boundaries and to have lost a sense of proportion.

That said, each departure had its own nature, character, dimension. During summer months, several boats a day come and go to Lavrion on the mainland. On one occasion I was going alone on the 6:00 a.m. boat and decided to walk down, partially for the exercise, but also because of the hassle of arranging taxi service at the ungodly hour (I learned quickly that the taxi drivers of Kea fit you into their schedule, not the other way around).

I left Hora on foot at 4:45 under a huge full moon that rained down silver all around me. It was a magical hour's walk–time apart from time, at least from daily time we know in daylight hours. There is an old stone way that is a shortcut down and thus which those walking favor. At that hour of the morning under the moon with the fresh aroma of the trees–lemon, olive, fig, pomegranate, and others–and the crisp calls of Kean owls in the distance, anything could have happened. And it could have been any time in the past. Minoan traders or Roman legions or Turkish warlords might have passed me. Nothing indicated the present for over a full mile of stone-paved pathway.

At the harbor, I watched the old ferry boat, the Ioulis II, slowly come to life as I sipped my Greek coffee at a kafeneon. I doubted that many would stir for the early boat mid-week. But I was wrong. Pickup trucks, vans, delivery trucks, construction trucks, German tourists in BMWs with boats in tow, Greeks in cars returning to Athens appeared from seemingly nowhere and lined up to back into the gaping entrance of the old tub. And islanders began to appear, carrying packages, overnight bags, flowers, gifts.

It took no more than fifteen minutes for the sleeping harbor to become busier than Athens' port of Pireaus at noon. And the reverse was equally true: by 6:10 the harbor was asleep again for several hours until the pale light beginning to appear behind Hora became another summer day.

Everywhere this rhythm of activity is the same. There are quiet hours, but when a place is busy, it is bustling. Even the smallest village becomes a metropolis in Greece at times with coming and going, talking and shouting, buying and selling. New Orleans is the largest port in the United States in terms of business done. But that work is nearly invisible, for one is barely conscious that so much commerce is taking place. Not so in Greece, or on Kea, where arrivals and departures punctuated the rush hours of each day.

Of the many departures, one other comes forth to be mentioned.

We were all three headed for Athens on an afternoon boat. We had asked about a bus to the boat and been told there would be one by one of the two bus drivers. Thus we made no arrangement for a taxi and arrived in the bus platea an hour before the boat's departure.

No bus. Several taxis came and went, and we made no effort to flag them down. "Nikos said there would be a bus, so we must wait," we said. But by 5:40 our chances of catching the boat some five miles down mountain looked impossible. We were angry. What Nikos had meant but not said was the "Perhaps the other bus will come." It did not, and since this was past summertime and a regular schedule, no one knew for certain when the bus would go anywhere.

We were almost resigned to skipping the boat (ah! a chance to delay a departure!), when I suggested we hitch. A Greek fellow had been caught in the same bind and had already started walking down to the parking area where a farmer was filling up plastic water containers and placing them in his pickup truck.

What the hell.

The farmer said no.

But then the Greek asked too, and we asked again, and he relented. It was a few miles out of his way, but...

Odette, Sam and the Greek squeezed into the cabin, and I rode in the open air in back, enjoying the scenery flying by as I had never done on the bus or in the taxis.

And we made the boat with thirty seconds to spare.

Cadillacs in the Sea

Bones are not all that falls into the sea. There are stones and cadillacs too.

The island of Milos, 1953: Spyros, now in his late fifties, returns to his home island after thirty years in America. He made a modest fortune with his bakery, but his wife is dead and he is thinking of settling down in the old home. He has also brought his eighteen-year-old son with him for a few months. The son hates the idea of Greece, though he has never been before.

As they arrive on a windy day on an old ferry, we see a primitive kind of pulley system as it hauls up a 1953 Cadillac and lowers it onto the quay. Everyone is there to admire this object of conspicuous consumption, knowing full well that there are no roads on the island for such a car. Spyros, nevertheless, has brought it to drive back and forth on the harbor front as a sign of his status.

The islanders soon learn that Spyros has a project in mind. Having made his money in business, he wants to make a contribution to archeology and the arts. What exactly? Well, since Venus de Milo came from the water around Milos, then surely there must be other statues too. He hires and outfits a boat to do some exploratory diving and searching, and takes on some unemployed fisherman and divers to crew the boat. The islanders laugh behind his back and cheat him on prices and such, but are thrilled to take his money.

Meanwhile, of course, while Spyros begins to become very disenchanted with the "new" Greece ("Greeks have lost all morals and sense of tradition since the War"), the son falls in love with a village girl and begins to enjoy himself.

Just as Spyros is ready to pack up and leave in disgust, a diver brings up another ancient statue. The islanders stop laughing. Spyros feels better, but is still packing. The son announces he wishes to stay a year "to remodel the old house." He has his arm around the village beauty. Spyros gives him his blessing.

As he is leaving, the same old ferry returns and begins to lift up the Cadillac with the rickety old pulley system. But the ropes snap and the Cadillac falls into the sea.

Two old fishermen have been observing all of this from a harborside cafe. One taps the other as he plays with his worry beads. "Eh, Niko, you see how life is? You take something from the sea, and you give something to the sea."

Spyros shrugs and leaves.

So went a story outline for a filmscript I cooked up years ago with a friend in Hollywood. We had been given twenty-four hours by a TV producer to come up with "something about a Greek who returns home from America in the 1950s but becomes disillusioned." Typical of American show biz, the producer listened to our idea, wrote copious notes, said he would "get back to us later," and then called the next day to say he didn't want our story or us and that he himself (who had never been to Greece) was going to write the script.

A year later it appeared as a TV movie starring Telly Savalas with many of our elements on the screen though the tale had been shifted from Milos to the mainland and the make of cars had been changed, so I've been told, for I've never seen it myself.

My friend and I, however, had also been stupid...or naive. We had not registered our idea (we had just thought it up hours before) and so had no legal recourse to our Greek island story.

I'm told the film was popular and reruns often late at night.

You can be sure that any movie ideas coming from our Kea experience will be registered immediately.

Blocking out and Taking in

The Old Man sat in his usual seat, tapped his cane and asked Kyria Poppy for another ouzo.

A radio in back of the kafeneon carried news that Soviet leader Gorbachev planned to visit Washington, D.C., in December to sign an arms reduction treaty with President Reagan.

"Young fellow," he said when he saw me. "Take a seat."

I did.

"I've been doing some more thinking since we last talked."

"Yes?"

"Yes. And I find there are two other types of people in the world."

Kyria Poppy brought the ouzo, and he motioned for her to bring me one as well.

"Soviets and Americans, that is, communists and capitalists?" I suggested, listening to the news.

"Not so important. No. I mean there are those who take in life and those who block it out."

"I don't completely follow," I said. My ouzo arrived.

"City folk, which includes you back home, spend much of their lives blocking out what's not wanted–noise, over stimulation for the eyeball, you know, so many ads, ugliness, and suffering too, beggars in the street–but city folk basically have to ignore them. Right? Otherwise, if you didn't block out how could you live in such a mess!"

"I see your point."

"But on Kea and rural places like Kea, it's different. We are free to take in, don't you know, the beauty of nature, the sounds of the village, the pleasures of the land and sea and sky. Simple, isn't it?" he laughed.

"From that perspective, I suppose so," I said.

"Yes. Either you open up to people and surroundings as we do, or you clam up and spend your life being suspicious and limited as city folk do." He paused to finish his drink. "So what does that make you now?"

"Something in between," I said, smiling.

Poppy came over, and I offered to pay for my drink and those of the Old Man. "What Old Man?" she said. "You are sitting by yourself!"

And I suddenly realized there were two other types of people in the world....

Apollo, Elias and Solar Energy

The major ancient temple on Kea, the one at Poles, was devoted to Apollo, the god of light and order among other characteristics. And certainly in the Cyclades, sunlight is in abundance most of the year. Thus the worship of Apollo is closely tied to respect for the god of the sun, Helios.

Christianity in its clever adaptation and adoption of many pagan gods and heroes transformed such sun worship into the Prophet Elias (Prophetis Elias). And so from Helios to Elias, Orthodox Greeks began to build mountaintop churches close to the sun, dedicated to the prophet who brought "light" to believers everywhere.

The twentieth century has seen yet another transformation. Solar energy has made it possible for individual families and homes to "praise" the sun and to benefit from such worship.

An important practical change I've noted in Greece in the years since I first arrived has been the steady and growing implementation of solar power on the local, house by house use.

An adequate solar unit for an average-sized house runs around a thousand dollars or less. And given the savings in electricity costs, such an investment is definitely a bargain for Greeks.

Solar panels do dot the roofs of Kean homes, not yet in the numbers of television aerials (roughly half the homes), but clearly a part of Greek life today that is here to stay.

Just think. Even the churches to Elias can now be operated by energy from the sun, that ageless power that has helped to make Greece so different from any other place on earth.

Even in modern times, the sun has inspired and animated Greek literature. Nikos Kazantzakis, for instance, dedicates his monumental sequel to Homer's

Odyssey to the Greek sun, in part, with these words:

> Above me spreads the raging sky, below me swoops
> my belly, a white gull that breasts the cooling waves:
> my nostrils fill with salty spray,
>> the billows burst swiftly against my back, rush on,
> and I rush after.
> Great Sun, who pass on high yet watch all things below.

Good Road

Our lives are always in between: between the sky and the earth, birth and death, joy and sorrow, tears and laughter, light and darkness, order and chaos.

Our time apart on Kea put us in touch with a place and a people who helped us, for the most part unknowingly, to see more clearly how even in these troubled contemporary times it is possible to live more fully "in between" without losing all sense of proportion in any one direction. For example: "The gods do not give to mankind all things at the same time," observes Homer. How true, how difficult, at times to accept.

Nikos Kazantzakis goes further to touch on the power of the Dionysian, beyond rationality and logic: "Every integral man has inside him, in his heart of hearts, a mystic center around which all else revolves. This mystic whirling lends unity to his thoughts and actions: it helps him find or invent the cosmic harmony…. Alas, for the man who does not feel himself governed inside by an absolute monarch. His ungoverned, incoherent life is scattered to the four winds."

Aristophanes echoes our close tie to nature, a joyful unity which is "comic," that is triumphant, in the broadest sense, a spirit we felt on Kea:

> "Earth is delighted now, peace is the voice of earth.
> Let each catch hands with his wife and dance his joy,
> Dance out his thanks, be grateful in music,
> And promise reformation with his heels."

Argiris and Vasso and the others we came to know on the island taught us, and wished us, the importance of a "good road." For the wish is not just about a going away, but for a safe return back to those you love and know as well.

"Good Road" to all!

To Petroussa and Back

"From here on summer nights," Argiris said, looking out over a placid sea below his family home at Petroussa, the southernmost tip of the island, "you can sit out here under the stars and watch the boats pass by, all lighted up like Christmas trees, and you can even hear clear as a bell all the music they happen to be playing."

It was the first Saturday in November, and we had at last connected with Argiris on a day in which to take in "his" part of the island.

Our time was running out, and I wanted to make good on his offer to travel with him to his home in the countryside. We had seen much of the island, but nothing of the southern tip except from the deck of the boat to Kithnos during August.

"Tomorrow," he had told us on Friday. "Is that alright?"

I was delighted.

We bent all our plans—not a difficult task—and by the appointed hour, 10:00 a.m., we were in front of his taverna ready to board his Toyota pickup truck, vintage 1977. He had originally scheduled departure for 7:00 a.m. but a call from a fisherman changed all of that. As a fishmonger as well as shopkeeper and taverna owner, Argiris would combine business and pleasure: Vasso, who had to stay behind and tend the taverna, would sell the freshly-caught marithes (smelt) at the shop, while we would sell them throughout the island on the way to Petroussa.

We had been through the worst weather winter could muster, and in all truthfulness, we were prepared for an equal bashing by the elements. But that day the wind disappeared, the sun shone, and temperatures danced in the low sixties. We felt Zeus or Apollo, the patron ancient god of the island, was being kind.

It was to be our single finest day on Kea.

The fact that Argiris even considered hauling the three of us, and of course Sam did come too, down the difficult roads to his family home we took as a warm gesture of acceptance. Argiris and Vasso were already "family" to us, and it was a good feeling that the feeling was reciprocal.

"What can you do?" Argiris muttered philosophically as we inched up the cliff above the village on a rock and dirt and mud road, the only kind we would know for all but the last ten kilometers of our return along the southern coast. "Though I am the fishmonger here, someone else beat me to it today. He hit the village and some of the countryside."

I sympathized. "Nothing to do. It happens. That's business," he said without a trace of bitterness, just a sigh of disappointment. "I bought thirty kilos of fish, and whatever I don't sell, I'll have to dump." And that was it. As usual, Argiris never cursed, never suggested he might even fantasize roughing up his competitor, who obviously knew exactly what he was doing in getting an hour's start on Argiris.

The map of Kea is terribly inaccurate. It shows a few roads, a few paths, nothing more. But in fact, the island is honeycombed with dirt roads of varying degrees of passibility, and more are built by the year, a fair number being private roads to solitary homes. Thus our trip to Petroussa was to be our only chance on Kea to explore multitudinous side roads leading here and there.

Our first road was a bust. The "other" fishmonger-for-a-day had been there, and although the inhabitants were full of sympathy, they were also full of fish.

We had to try elsewhere.

The next road, leading deep into Pera Meria, the northeast side of the island with a spectacular rugged coastline, unlike the more gentle western coast, was more successful.

Argiris' sales tactics were simple. He'd pull up to a house or a clump of houses and shout out his window in a strong, resonant base voice, "FRESH FISH: BLACK MARITHES." It worked. Out of nowhere, hobbling women, old men, young wives, workers from the field appeared, peered into the side by side boxes of fish under canvas in the metal sink-like container in the back of the truck, and then called out for one or two or sometimes three or four kilos, often buying for other relatives or friends they felt sure were low on smelts. (The fact is, those living in the interior are treated to such a round of fresh fish only once a week at best, thus the strong showing of individuals out of nowhere throughout the island.)

Sam loved it.

We'd bump along the road a bit, halt, shout, get out, sell and talk, get back in, and continue along. The sun shone, the fish diminished, and we were treated to scenery we had not seen before.

"Was all the fish Argiris sold caught by Keans, or more properly, `Tsians,' after the unofficial name of the island `Tsia'"? "Yes," he replied," but we only have three fisherman and they're old. That's why we don't get a lot of variety. Marithes are easy to catch and you don't have to go far out. But in the old days, there were lots of fishermen here. However, even then, not so many were from Kea. Many were xenoi."

"Xenoi?"

"Not from Kea, from the mainland, many from across the way in Lavrion."

Again that word and its meaning. Greeks not from Kea were xenoi too!

By 2:00 p.m. we had climbed the slopes of Mt. Saint Simeon. Still a brilliant day, and tempting coves and beaches appeared below us along the coast, and well-kept scattered farm houses dotted the area we drove through.

One stop was to the home of some of Argiris' cousins. Everyone—grandmother, wife, two children, and later, husband and another relative—showed up to talk and buy. And the charming little girl (age six?) helped herself to some of the smallest fish in the back to feed her two delighted cats.

Another customer was a lively old woman in a solid stone home with a square windmill next to the house run by metallic blades on top of the roof blowing horizontally. Where did she get such an unusual, but, come to think of it, intelligent design? "My son is a metal worker, so . ."

It didn't take us too many stops before we realized something we had not known before and which Argiris confirmed: that the houses in the countryside were generally spiffier, larger and better equipped with televisions, fridges and other recently purchased appliances.

"But I had been led to believe that many people here made their home in Hora their number one house, and only semi-"camped out" in the countryside."

"No, no!" said Argiris. "For most, but not all, it's just the opposite. They live out here. The home in Hora is generally for market days, special occasions, holidays. That's one reason why the village looks so empty at night."

He had a point. Of course absent landlords in Athens and abroad accounts for a good quarter of the homes (a guess), yet I had not considered that the scarcity of lights at night was because the owners were living throughout the rest of the island, happy to spend only special days in Hora!

By 3:00 every fish had been sold!

Argiris smiles. "Bad start, strong finish," he laughed. "But in business, you never know."

We now pointed the Toyota on the roughest stretch of road yet, the one to Petroussa.

Odette, like Sam, felt how special the day had become, even though she did not understand Greek and waited patiently for my updates on what had been said. It did not matter, however. The scenery, the people, the island opened up before us. Yes we had made the trip to Poles for the paneyeri, and, yes, I had done some jogging in remote places. But we would never have seen so many back roads, homes, views, farm folk, if it had not been for Argiris' invitation.

While the central region of the island is full of scattered homes always in view, the road to Petroussa showed us not a single home in sight.

"How did you get started in the taverna business," I asked.

"That was ten years ago. The fine old guy who ran it died, and Vasso and I thought it over and decided to take it over. We already had the grocery which I had taken over from an uncle who ran it for years. But like everybody else, I still have fields and trees and a few animals as well. Not to mention selling the fish! Keeps me busy!"

On a rocky, barren stretch, Argiris pulled over and parked. "We're here...almost."

There was nothing around.

But Argiris grabbed the precooked food prepared by Vasso, and we headed up a small path and over a ridge. Roughly a mile later, Sam on my shoulders as usual, we came upon his old family home: a simple two-roomed whitewashed farmhouse with a covered alcove between the two rooms.

Beyond the house was the view of the straits between Kea and Kithnos, a main traffic route, with seldom fewer than two ships in view at a time.

Quail called out in hollows near by.

Sheep belonging to Argiris' family dotted the nearest ridge.

Wildflowers blew in the light wind.

Sam became immediately absorbed in following the adventures of the three or four cats that go with the house.

And we were met by Costa.

Costa?

Argiris' brother. 49 years old, deaf and mute and alone. He has lived year after year at Petroussa, as a shepherd, farm keeper, modern hermit of sorts.

He was overjoyed to see us. Though he couldn't talk and had not had the chance to learn sign language properly, he said all through his eyes and his animated gestures.

Costa was not crazy.

This caught me off guard. I don't know exactly what I expected. But from the moment several months before when we learned that Argiris had a deaf-mute brother at the tip of the island living alone, we knew he had to be "different" in many ways.

No. He was not crazy, not done in by years of solitude, isolation, relentless contact with the elements. The original Robinson Crusoe, Alexander Selkirk, or course, was quite mad when found on his island, unlike Defoe's fantasy novel which would have him becoming a one-man British colony (yes, there was Friday, but he was a black slave, and thus, in Robinson's eyes, not on his level at all).

Costa was in fact, the most child-like adult I have met. The magic of discovery, of expression without verbal language but with body language and visual language is there in rich abundance. An abundance that most of us have never known. He could say much that I could not begin to say.

Was he deprived? Yes. At best, he was making the most of a more than tough life. The location was spectacular, the view overwhelming. But to live it day in and day out alone, without electricity, running water, or a road, places Costa in a most unusual category.

Their father had been worse than a bastard towards Costa, and yet Argiris did not say it in those words. In his ever gentle way, the strongest attack he could make on his old man was to say that, "Father was of the Old School." He then explained that as a child, Costa had been contacted by the queen at that time, Frederika, and offered a year's free schooling at a special academy for the deaf in Athens. The father had torn up the certificate and ended Costa's one chance to escape the prison of his silence. Argiris' implication was that Costa never knew about the letter.

That makes Costa's solitude tragic, not really heroic.

But above all, he is a survivor. He is there, living, close to his animals, to the sea, the wind, the sun, the birds.

Vasso had packed a feast and so, within a few minutes of arriving, in the covered alcove, we feasted. Broiled chicken, feta cheese, cabbage salad, wine, marithes, and pomegranates which we cracked open and bit into the hundreds of rich pulpy seeds.

Costa was excited to have guests and "talked" the whole meal, sharing encounters with rabbits, wild dogs and such with us, via Argiris' sympathetic translations. Their relationship was a strong friendship. Argiris understood Costa and Costa trusted Argiris. They could speak each other's language.

Sam took to Costa immediately, as well. And there was never a single question about "why doesn't that man talk." Sam liked him, felt his spontaneity, his warmth, his directness, his connectedness and that was that.

Odette fought back tears the rest of the afternoon. The day had brought us treasures. But Costa broke our hearts. How to embrace both extremes? How to comprehend such beauty and such injustice at once was the double-edged emotion of joy and pain we experienced.

Argiris was as good natured as ever. He made no special effort to apologize, analyze, explain his brother. It was as if in accepting us and thus in bringing us down to see and share his home, he felt we would understand. And we did, even if we had trouble accepting Costa's situation.

Odette and Sam played in the yard while Argiris talked of his childhood. "School was in Kato Meria for the elementary years. That meant a three-hour walk up and three hours back." He laughed his good humored laugh again. "In the winter that could be difficult, and in the spring there were temptations along the way," was all he said. I knew the road and could judge the distance. He was not exaggerating.

I looked inside the spartan rooms. One was a bedroom with a double and two singles. A chest or two. A few faded photos. That was almost all. The other was the kitchen, winter living room. His complete kitchenware consisted of a few plates, a few pots, a couple of forks and spoons, and a gas burner. But what did he eat as a steady diet? We had brought lunch. Where was his food? And what did he do besides tend the farm? "He's afraid of the propane lamp," Argiris said when I pointed to it. That limited him to a simple kerosene lamp, no television, and a life without being able to read. What did he do?

Neither Odette nor I could begin to imagine his life. Costa was living beyond our experience, in another realm. A territory on the fringes of human experience, part holy, part visionary, part imaginary, part lonely, part self-contained. Life in Hora had for us modern city folk been an exercise in simplifying. But Costa's life at the end of the island on a cliff with a view that takes your breath away but an isolation which would soon drive us mad for sure, was an extreme we were not able to fathom.

The winter afternoon was dimming.

We had to leave.

Costa gestured.

"You must come back. Stay longer. Stay a week, or two!" said Argiris.

"Yes," I said, without hesitation. "Yes!"

And I meant it.

Something had changed for us in Petroussa.

"If we left Kea without this day," Odette said when we returned, exhausted, sunburnt, happy, and sad but not depressed, "We still would have felt it was all worth while. But today..."

She then shared the same problem I felt keenly. My words were not adequate to express all that Petroussa had suggested to us.

Argiris had taken us out for a trip, but it had become a journey. One we would continue to live over and over again.

A Full and Intense Life

Greece and the Greeks should not be idealized. Besides the astonishing amount of culture and science and political structure they passed on to us, they also had their darker side, their exploitation of slaves, women, minorities, or each other as seen in civil wars, regretted emotional decisions, foolish undertakings.

Life on Kea simply reinforced this point. Certainly we came to appreciate many factors and attributes of Kean life while also being frustrated and angered by yet other traits (of course one must take into account one's own biased culture-bound perspective when living in another society).

"We can be a ridiculous people," the writer Antonis Samarakis told me near the end of our stay, the last time I met him in an island-like small kafeneon hidden in the heart of Athens. "We can be selfish, mean, corrupt, petty, snobbish and stupid."

"But would you live anywhere else?"

"Of course not!" Samarakis said with a smile. "Because the common man has his good points, especially in Greece."

In a real sense, it is not the Greeks who are at fault for building a hazy, idealized vision of "Hellas." Foreigners over the centuries have manufactured an unrealistic and romantic notion of what Classical Greece was like, an image that not only distorted the past but damaged the present as many Philhellines saw fit to dismiss modern Greeks as corrupted inferiors to the pure Greeks of old. But the fact is even in classical Greece, no pure race existed. Greece is and was a crossroads of East and West, gaining from the unique blending of each, philosophically, religiously, culturally, racially.

A more balanced view of the Greeks is represented in these words by a scholar: "In a world of which the Greeks knew the somber no less than the bright side, they lived a full and intense life. It was not laborious nor always honest, and instead of serving the community, the citizens had begun to live on it, but in their economic as well as in their political life, they always tended to make the most of things." (Victor Ehrenberg, *The People of Aristophanes*. New York, 1962)

These words refer to Greece in its decline at the beginning of the 4th century B.C. But they apply to Greece today as well. For better and for worse, one feels the intensity and fullness with which Greeks live their lives.

And must of this has to do, I feel, with their firm acceptance and understanding of the brevity of life. If not bones in the sea, we do become bones in the ground or, in the case of cremation, in the fire. Period. "Man's life is like the shadow of smoke," as Sophocles wrote. But within that brief bright flame, much can happen.

Living on Kea, I realized even more sharply how a similar awareness is part of life in New Orleans, which, like Greece, is a rich mixture of heritages from differing cultures. One of New Orleans' best loved musical bands puts it best perhaps. In a recent interview, Aaron Neville, the lead singer of the Neville Brothers, a black rhythm and blues band with strong New Orleans' roots, said, "You don't hear no noise coming from the graveyard, bro...so while you got it, you better use it!"

Greetings

There are far more greetings in Greek than in American English. The breakdown of our ability to develop much of a span of phrases to connect with each other is represented in the bland neutrality of "have a nice day."

Of course in Greek there are the expected greetings:

How are you?: Ti kanete?

What's new?: Ti nea?

And good morning (kalimera), good evening (kalispera) and good night (kali nichta).

But on Kea I became more aware than I had been living years ago in Athens of how many other expressions there are depending on occasion and time of the year.

I remembered using "good month" (kalo mena) at the beginning of each month, a fine way to acknowledge the beginning of another span of thirty days. Yet on Kea I was frequently wished "good week" as well (kali evthomatha) on Mondays, a saying I fully plan to attempt to introduce to English! And, from August 16th through roughly the middle of October, people wished each other "good winter" (kali heimona).

Then there was the one I heard every day: "good digestion" (kali oreksi) which we have in English but do not use frequently. Why? Well, certainly in a nation of fast food junkies such a greeting said over a hamburger and fries eaten on the run makes no sense, but in a country where the big meal is in the middle of the day, followed by a siesta, it does!

My favorite expression, however, which I had not heard before coming to Kea was a wish for any travels: "good road" (kalo dromo). Not bon voyage, but a good road. Kalo Dromo. Greeks have always been voyagers. The Odyssey isn't just about Odysseus: its about all Greeks, and so "good road" is a heartfelt wish.

Life Without a Time Table

A letter from a Yugoslav friend reminded us how different our time on Kea was for us and for our friends who, like most people, followed a daily routine. In part, the letter went like this:

"Dear Andy,

I've made a big mistake. I was about to write you in New Orleans, but reading your last letter, I realized you leave the Cyclades in late November(!?). This mistake of mine is typical for Yugoslav intellectual-proletarian: we can't imagine that somebody can spend more than 20 days at sea-side not going back to the office!"

We thought a lot about what it means to take time apart from routine. For us, it proved to be an experience that opened unexpected possibilities for us and within us. We could begin to see more clearly how much what we think is necessary is not, and how much attitudes and activities that do not get much attention during the fast-paced existence according to a set time schedule, take on more pressing urgency when one jumps off the roller coaster. And our extended time on Kea helped us also realize that even a summer vacation is often not long enough to allow people a chance to gain fresh perspectives and new energy for what they (we) consider important.

But talks with our friends everywhere brought to light another realization. Some people, of course, would be afraid to break out of their routine. A set schedule is a kind of security. If offers comfort, similarity, continuity, and freedom from being challenged or unduly upset. Yet other friends truly enjoyed their. routines and so could not imagine breaking away from home, job, community.

"I know I'm working too hard," said an artist friend in New York, "but it's what I want to do! I can't imagine that anything else could make me happier."

And a well-known filmmaker about whom I've written frequently sounds a similar though less enthusiastic note, "If I weren't working on a film, I'd feel guilty. Two weeks off the job is about all I can take!" (Note: He is Catholic!)

Of course, some would like to take off but feel they cannot. In some cases this may be true. But life on Kea suggested to us that if you want time apart from routine, you can find some way to work it out.

Much has to do with the over emphasis on career and work that exists in the United States. Americans do, by and large, work very hard. No wonder foreign friends have remarked after visiting the States that they couldn't possibly keep up with an American work schedule and enjoy their lives too!

My time apart was made possible by a sabbatical. It's a concept–time off with pay–that has come under fire as the economy creaks along and administrators look for corners to cut. But while some universities are cutting back on or cutting sabbaticals out all together, ironically, a number of businesses are beginning to see the value of time apart from routine. The constant complaint of "executive burnout" is a very real problem for corporations, but it is a burden to many more, I suspect, than would care to admit it.

One book years ago suggested that teachers would be better if required to work at a job totally unrelated to their teaching specialty one year out of every three! Of course, that's rather extreme. Or is it? What if politicians could only be on the job for a couple of years and then would be forced to take time apart? And what if we added, as in our example, a geographic component? "From this day on, all senators must spend one in four years in a state other than their home state and in a capacity unrelated (directly) to their services as elected officials."

Impossible! Unthinkable! Too romantic!

But without such proposals, how will things begin to change?

In reality, time apart, should appear in many forms. One final example has long interested me as a father of two. I am speaking of the dismal provisions for maternity leave in the United States. A few weeks, maybe a month if you are lucky. But in many countries, especially the socialist block, women have up to a year or even two with their child, a good part of that with pay and with a guarantee of their jobs when they return. How often we have heard American friends who have children say, "I plan to be back to work in two weeks." Why miss the first year of your child's life punching the clock at the same pace, with no provisions either for part-time or for full-time off with security.

But I would change things even further as a father when elected president(!). Paternity leave should be an option as well. It exists in countries such as Yugoslavia, though, granted, few ever take advantage of it (patriarchal structures die hard, despite good intentions). If parents are allowed a year off, for instance, one way of cutting the pie would be for the wife to take the first six months off to nurse and enjoy the child, and the husband the second half of the year. Or nine months and three. It doesn't matter. What does matter, however, is the need for rethinking unscheduled time off as a constructive part of our over scheduled lives.

For the most part, those who say they could not imagine taking time off are friends in the arts who more or less work for themselves anyway. In a sense, they are already apart.

My remarks are, therefore, more appropriately aimed for those who, like myself, work for someone else at set times for a set wage. It is, once again, a fact of ancient Greek culture that leisure time and constructive free time made discourse and creativity and philosophy possible. If one is too tired at night to do anything but watch cable TV and eat fast food, I question how much pleasure one can really be experiencing, how fully one can be living.

The Greeks tell of the American businessman in a three-piece suit who comes up to a simple Greek fisherman sitting barefoot at a seaside cafe drinking his ouzo in the late afternoon. "Costa," says the American, "I've been watching you and I have some suggestions to make. Yes, you support your family adequately with your fishing, but listen. If you fish an extra hour a day, you would bring in enough fish to make more money and in a year buy a second boat. With that, by the same method, you would have five boats in three years. Soon you would have a fleet. Then you could build a fish processing plant. And in no time, say, fifteen years, you would be rich, you could do anything you wished to do. For instance, simply sit and watch the sea if you wanted." "But I can sit and watch the sea right now," says the fisherman. "Why should I wait fifteen years and work myself to death!"

Mermaids and Rainbows

We never saw any mermaids near Kea.

But on the day before we left, there was a double rainbow arched across the island. Scientifically, it was just a certain refraction of light and color through the winter sky, but for us, it was a sign, a message, a grand gesture.

We had been away almost a week and had returned on the 16th of November for our last few days before departing for the States.

Odette had fully made up her mind not to return to the island should the weather even closely resemble the bitter storm we had survived just a week before. But on that balmy Monday, the weather could not have been better. We sailed "home" to Kea on the old Ioulis II tub of a boat on a mirror-like sea under a pale blue sky. Temperatures hovered between the high fifties at night and touched into the seventies during the day.

We didn't want to leave.

Just in the few days we had been gone the island had undergone a remarkable transformation. The baked brown hues we had known for months had given way to rich greens. Olives were dark black-purple, weighing down branches, ready to be harvested. Orange groves were almost ripe enough for gathering. Flowers we had not seen before were out everywhere.

In the midst of winter, a first spring had appeared.

That next-to-the-last day gave us the complete range of an island winter experience. I awoke early to a mixed sunny and cloudy sky. By midmorning a torrential downpour and thunderstorm enveloped all of Hora sending rivers of rain down the streets and lanes for the first time. An hour later almost all clouds disappeared, and a clear winter sun shone warm.

A hike and a final swim?

Both seemed easy goals on such a day.

And so we set out on foot for the harbor and beach. Sam was in great spirits as well, especially when he discovered that his beloved blackberries were still around, albeit in greatly reduced numbers. Everywhere we looked, we felt as if we were seeing a new island for the first time. Green to the left of us, to the right, in front, behind, down below and far above. Greece had surprised us again. Even for me, this sudden growth was unexpected. Yes, I have memories of fertile Decembers under mild skies before the harsh storms of January roll in. But I did not remember the speed of change. It was like a miracle.

Swimming was still on our agenda, but by the time we reached the harbor, we were hungry. "No problem," said Odette. "Let's eat, then swim." Yet by the time we had finished a simple meal of goat in lemon sauce, country salad and a special kind of meatball, the day had shifted radically once more.

The wind had risen, churning the rippleless sea we had seen just minutes before. The sky turned a deep, dark, threatening hue. But patches of brilliant light shone through illuminating small, shifting areas of the coast in exciting high contrasts. The harbor village itself took on an intensely cubist look, as bright light caught one side of a whitewashed wall, but not the other. We had never seen anything quite like it.

Then the rains came again.

But as the afternoon boat sailed in, one rainbow, and then its twin, arose, spilling from the sky into the brightly repainted ship. Odette could not take her eyes away from the scene. "It's…beautiful," she said. But somehow, we felt that beauty much deeper than our words could express. We had been happy on Kea and we had had our share of obstacles as well. Island life had not been paradise, whatever that is, but it had given us chances we had longed for and surprises we would not forget.

We rode the bus up to Hora with only two others aboard. The rainbows shifted as we moved. At one moment the band of colors fell into the isolated church built by the Two Sisters in memory of their well-loved grandfather. Another time it curved over fields, and finally it spanned directly into Hora itself.

Not even the crowd of silent mourners gathered in the bus platea on their way back from a makarea meal after another funeral at the taverna across from Argiris' could dampen our lifted spirits. Grief too, we felt, must surely be part of joy.

Bye Bye, Kea

Odette and Sam left the day before I did on an extremely blustery day. In fact, I was surprised the old Ioulis II sailed out of the harbor in such a wind at all. Once Sam and Odette and Argiris, with whom they were catching a ride to Athens, were inside the boat, I turned and noticed a small plastic-fiberglass fishing boat blowing down the street, end over end. It took two men to hold it down.

As Sam went on board, he turned and said, "Bye bye, Kea. See you soon!"

I had jogged down to the harbor to see them off and, for the first time, I jogged back as well with a large, perhaps mile-wide rainbow in front of me.

I stayed the extra day to clean up and to finish up a new screenplay I had written on Kea about an American teenage boy and a Greek teenage girl–young woman who become friends while he is attempting to "borrow" a statue from the museum in Thessaloniki as a last gift for a dying relative. For besides the family time and hours spent outside swimming and hiking and being with friends, Kea had also been my first chance ever to have a string of months together for uninterrupted writing and reading. Both for my screenwriting and my academic work, the peace of Kea offered me what I had long hoped for: freedom from fragmentation and of having a day chopped into a million fragments of responsibilities, interests, and chores.

That last night an icy wind and rain lashed the island. Before supper, I took Sam's simple tricycle which we had bought for his island stay, over to Prokopis' house. Prokopis was the small Greek boy Sam's age we had met at the beginning of our stay, riding a donkey. Sam had never forgotten his ride on a separate donkey beside Prokopis that day. His parents were happy to see me, grateful for the bike, and ushered me into their Spartan home to sit at the round dining room table where I was served by the younger of the two teenage daughters I had talked with a month before about teen life on the island. I did not wish to stay yet I did not want to offend them. Thus I managed to depart after a glass of local wine and half a plate of octopus stew.

The rains had not let up.

Dripping wet, I entered Argiris' taverna. There in front of the television sat Costa, Argiris' brother from Petroussa. He smiled, jumped up, shook my hand, beaming with good will, and making a number of energetic gestures to Vasso who translated with ease. "He wants you to come back and spend two weeks or longer!" she said.

"Tell him I promise I will return," I said. And meant it. Costa tapped his heart and smiled. And then began to make fun of the television show, a documentary from England on the dangers of AIDs.

"Can Costa read Greek?"

"No," replied Vasso working on my cabbage salad. "He was never in school long enough to learn." Somehow I had not taken this in before. So it now struck me how totally isolated he was. He could not read the paper or understand the subtitles on the screen about the dangers of making love without taking strong precautions.

There were only the three of us that evening and the storm outside. Over Vasso's splendid lamb chops, salad and fresh beans, washed down with half a bottle of white wine, we talked and laughed and thought about future visits we hoped to make to Kea. I also jokingly, but seriously, suggested they could open a branch "franchise" in New Orleans which Vasso vetoed. "I never thought I would live to say this because I once longed to live in Athens, which I have done," she said, "but you couldn't drag me from Kea now!"

My last morning on the island was clear, calm, bright, warm.

I rose early and worked, then walked through the village to the post office. The last letter I received was from my mother: she reported happily that my grandmother who had been ill and even suspected of having cancer was better and had been cleared of the possibility of cancer. That was good news indeed.

And as I walked up the main street, the women were walking down towards the butcher shops carrying two poles between them with dozens of juicy island sausages hanging from them. I turned immediately and followed. Argiris had told me that the Kean sausage was special, but that they did not begin to make it until after the first storms of winter. But here they were! I bought two kilos—four and a half pounds—as soon as they reached the shop.

Before locking the house, I took one more look around for any left items. The place was clean and silent and too empty now that we had packed up and moved out, but especially empty because Sam was not running around to tell us about a snail on the porch or to ask if he could mix honey and peanut butter again to make peanut butter balls.

Since I did not have much to carry, I decided to walk down to the boat.

The weather had never been clearer. Not only could I see the mainland and the island of Eubea, but even, for the first time from our house, a touch of the island of Andros as well.

The island was now dark green with winter vegetation and the air was fragrant with lemon and thyme and other plants.

Children played in the school yard, filling the village with happy sounds.

And with my portable typewriter in one hand and my ragged knapsack I had kept since high school full of books, a few clothes, a toothbrush and half a bottle of Jim Beam bourbon bought a few weeks before in Hungary during a brief visit, I started down the mountain, the sea before me and Hora behind.

We would be back.

"Kalo dromo," villagers who saw me called out.

Then I was on the boat and we were headed out to sea.

Another journey had begun. The salty tang of the sea breeze as we churned through the pale blue water tasted fine.

I thought of Archilochos' words and how life for the Greeks begins and ends with the sea:

> Decks awash,
> Mast-top dripping,
> And all
> Balanced on the keen edge
> Now of the wind's sword,
> Now of the wave's blade.

Postscript 1996

Hot and dusty and Argiris struggled some 75 yards, much to my complete amazement, down a stoney mountainside from his pick up truck to the old family home in Petroussa where his deaf brother Costa still lives. He struggled, because on his back he carried a refrigerator for Costa.

There was still no electricity down at this beautiful but barren tip of Kea. Thus the fridge was one of those designed to work off of bottled gas.

Costa saw us coming and left the circular stone-lined threshing floor where he was working three mules over the summer crop of wheat, pounding out the grain from the chaff in the ageless custom that one so rarely sees performed anymore in Greece.

It felt good to come back to Petroussa.

But this was the summer of 1993 and six years had gone by since we had last been to Petroussa..

The summer of 1993 we returned as a family and lived in the same house in Hora we had lived in during 1987. Some changes were immediately apparent. Sam was now eight and a half and we now had a lively daughter, Caroline, who was three and a half. Sam remembered very little from those days of 1987, so this recent summer meant that we enjoyed Kea once more with fresh eyes as both children experienced it for the "first" time.

Other changes had occurred.

Judy and Lou had separated, but Judy kept the house we rented and Lou held on to the older house next door. Their beautiful daughter, Eirene, at thirteen, was truly both Greek and American, playing a tough game of soft ball, more than holding her own on the trombone, and hanging out with the neighborhood Greeks on the island when she is here, speaking Greek perhaps even more fluently than English.

And the island itself.

Even from a distance as the new ferry boat (larger/faster) approaches the harbor you can see the growing number of summer homes being thrown up all over the island. In short, Kea has been truly discovered by Athenians with money to burn on weekend retreats. But the number of foreign tourists remains low. Thus while Greek tourism was down some 20-30% during the summer of 1993 because of the Bosnian War (particularly German tourists who used to drive down through the former Yugoslavia), those on Kea claimed they saw no significant dip themselves.

The increase in villas and pensions along the coast and dotting the hills along the coast has meant, of course, an increase in traffic. Cars, motorcycles, trucks crowd the ferry boat and keep the coastal roads buzzing.

Up in Hora, however, the boom is not as obvious. What we did notice were other signs of the times. Leading all of these was the fact that Vasso and Argiris, after nineteen years of running their taverna, had decided to close down.

They both looked fine. Argiris' hair is a pleasing grey-white now and his features even more handsome with the years. And Vasso's eyes are even more gentle now that she is not as exhausted as she once was, sometimes working more than 24 hours straight when farmers used to come to town and spend a whole day drinking and eating nonstop.

Why close? Health, primarily. Vasso has suffered from being on her feet so many years and her circulation is not good. But it's also the times. Three trendy tavernas have opened up including one of which–near the bus/taxi plaza–which serves gyro–the Greek equivalent of the fast food hamburger. But the locals have stopped coming too. With markets becoming more active all over the island, there is not the same rhythm of the Sunday market morning in Hora as being the major market day. So on those evenings that we were fortunate enough to eat at Argiris and Vasso's (they still stayed open this summer on weekends for those who asked), we were often the only ones there.

This did not mean that they have become idle, however. Remember that everyone seems to have several jobs on the island. And for Argiris this means running the grocery store across from the taverna, being the major fishmonger on the island, and tending to his own farm which includes tending his bees to gather the excellent honey this island produces.

Furthermore he is not alone. Their daughter, Eirene, married a handsome young fellow from the mainland, Costa, and they live together in a very well laid out and equipped apartment upstairs from Argiris and Vasso. And both help with the shop and, sometimes, the taverna whenever it is open. (Until it is sold, they will apparently open it for special occasions including funeral meals.)

And our old general store nearby our house, Yannis, is still run by Yannis and his family. What had changed was that Yannis now had a granddaughter Sam's age, Haralena, with whom both Sam and Caroline could play in the narrow street in front of the store.

Once more, neither Odette nor I had to worry. The kids would simply go up and down as they pleased and were very happy to run errands to Yannis or even down to Argiris' and back.

Happily, the sense of festivity continues to survive and thrive. We were here for the feast day of the island in early June when tables were set out in the platea (the square) and the local fiddle player, who now has his own CD and tape of his music, played from ll p.m. to 9 a.m. almost nonstop. And as we fell asleep that night hearing his fiddle echo throughout the village, it seemed clear how similar such music seemed to the folk fiddle anywhere, from the bayous of Louisiana to the plains of Hungary.

And there was another custom we had never witnessed before. It was the evening of the first day of summer and suddenly little fires appeared to be lit throughout the village. Sam could not believe it and went running out to see what was going on. Men, and some women too, had set fire to the Easter flower wreaths everyone makes and puts over their doors. Not only that, they were jumping over the burning wreaths and dancing. Why? A tradition for good luck.

Roads too have been improved.

This is especially true of the back road to the monastery of Kastriani. But it seems only a matter of a few years before many of the island back roads are paved. "And don't think they will do it because of tourism," commented Lou. "It's the common market fund that is interested because of all the milk and meat on the island. The farmers need to get their product to market more effectively."

The monastery has also been done over and upgraded. Freshly painted and now under the watchful care of a young married couple, Anna and Yannis, for four months of the year, this very attractive location with perhaps the most stunning view on the island, is now open for travellers and tourists alike to sleep over, eat, rest. We tested it out this summer staying in a remodeled room with a balcony and private bath. Food was simple–Greek meatballs, an eggplant dish and french fries for supper–but tasty and at $25 a night for a family of four, who could ask for more?

⟨⟩⟨⟩

Argiris somehow negotiated the 75 yards with the fridge and set it down in the courtyard of the house. Vasso had come on this trip too on this hot July afternoon and had brought a feast of chicken and pasta, country salad and "gigantes"–those delicious large beans in a tomato sauce–bread and wine and fresh cheese which Costa had prepared.

Once the fridge was in place and Sam and Caroline had discovered where the chickens, cats, dogs, goats, and donkeys were, we feasted. Then there was the obligatory long siesta. We stretched out in one of the two rooms while Argiris, Costa and Vasso took the other. As I fell asleep I looked up at the simple whitewashed walls and took in the ikons, the faded black and white family photos, the old calendars still hanging as if the years did not matter, and a picture of Donald Duck and Goofy, somehow appropriate as a 20th-century ikon of childish fantasy adding a lighter, more playful touch to everything else.

And there was the silence broken only by the noisy scratching of cicadas outside.

This was the peace we had found years ago visiting Costa.

And it was still here. Unbroken, complete, real.

After the nap we had our coffee and watched Costa delight in showing Sam and Caroline more things–ancient pottery and pretty stones he had found plus a wind-up doll he had rescued from the sea. What was clear was that he delighted in being with them and they loved being with him. "I don't want to leave this place," said Sam. "We don't need electricity either, do we?" said three-year-old Caroline.

The war in Bosnia and the million other crises in the world were in progress in 1993 and show no signs of disappearing. But here in Petroussa, centuries away from the rest of the world, a Homeric tranquility reigns still.

We returned again in 1994 and stayed in the harbor, an experience we had never had before. Yes, we missed the self-enclosed sense of Hora, and, yes, we missed the incomparable view of the whole Aegean spread out before us. But there were advantages for the children especially. Sam and Caroline could walk directly from our small rented home to the beach and play, swim, meet other children.

And in 1995, I came back alone for two evenings in August which included the Feast of the Virgin on the 15th, a night of dancing and feasting throughout the night. I was surprised to see that not only was there live music in Hora as usual, but in the harbor as well. A new shore side taverna had opened, and the traditional dances went on all night and as I left on the early boat the next day, the musicians were still playing.

Best of all, I had shared a large feast with Argiris and Vasso once more. But not in the taverna which only opens now for special occasions. Rather, they invited me to their home and rolled out an endless supply of lamb, salad, fish, vegetables, fruits and wine. We laughed over old times and shared our concerns about the present–in Greece and the Balkans including Bosnia.

And then Argiris drove me back to the harbor where I was staying for the night in a small hotel since I knew every other place was packed for the festival. Argiris was shaking his head: "You shouldn't stay in a hotel," he said.

He turned and smiled.

"Because you know you can always stay at our home since you are like a brother, a member of the family."

And I smiled too.

For I felt it was true.

Kea was and will be a second home for me, Odette, Sam and Caroline.

About the Author

Andrew Horton is a professor of film and literature at Loyola University New Orleans, an award-winning screenwriter, and founding director of the Aegean Institute. He is the author of twelve books and many articles including a book of translations of modern Greek plays and essays on Greek humor, cinema and culture. He and his family live in New Orleans and visit Greece frequently, often as the leader of student summer session abroad programs.

Horton has lived in Greece for more than seven years, speaks Greek, and has visited more than 50 islands.

Odette, Sam, Andy and Phil Horton on their Kea balcony, July 1987.

Printed in the United States
54126LVS00005B/307-339